STUDENT UNIT GUIDE

NEW EDITION

AQA A2 Business Studies Unit 4

The Business Environment and Managing Change

Gwen Coates

Series editor: John Wolinski

PHILIP ALLAN

Philip Allan, an imprint of Hodder Education, an Hachette UK company,
Blenheim Court, George Street, Banbury, Oxfordshire OX16 5BH

Orders
Bookpoint Ltd, 130 Milton Park, Abingdon, Oxfordshire OX14 4SB
tel: 01235 827827
fax: 01235 400401
e-mail: education@bookpoint.co.uk
Lines are open 9.00 a.m.–5.00 p.m., Monday to Saturday, with a 24-hour message answering service.
You can also order through the Philip Allan Updates website: www.philipallan.co.uk

© Gwen Coates 2012

ISBN 978-1-4441-4809-1

First printed 2012
Impression number 5
Year 2017 2016 2015

Cover photo: GP/Fotolia

Printed in Dubai

Hachette UK's policy is to use papers that are natural, renewable and recyclable products and made
from wood grown in sustainable forests. The logging and manufacturing processes are expected to
conform to the environmental regulations of the country of origin.

Contents

Content Guidance

Questions & Answers

Getting the most from this book

Examiner tips
Advice from the examiner on key points in the text to help you learn and recall unit content, avoid pitfalls, and polish your exam technique in order to boost your grade.

Knowledge check
Rapid-fire questions throughout the Content Guidance section to check your understanding.

Knowledge check answers
1 Turn to the back of the book for the Knowledge check answers.

Summary

Summaries
- Each core topic is rounded off by a bullet-list summary for quick-check reference of what you need to know.

Questions & Answers

Exam-style questions

Examiner comments on the questions
Tips on what you need to do to gain full marks, indicated by the icon **e**.

Sample student answers
Practise the questions, then look at the student answers that follow each set of questions.

Examiner commentary on sample student answers
Find out how many marks each answer would be awarded in the exam and then read the examiner comments (preceded by the icon **e**) following each student answer. Annotations that link back to points made in the student answers show exactly how and where marks are gained or lost.

AQA A2 Business Studies

About this book

This guide has been written to support your revision for AQA A2 Business Studies Unit 4: The Business Environment and Managing Change. It is divided into two sections: Content Guidance and Questions & Answers.

The **Content Guidance** section offers concise coverage of Unit 4, combining an overview of key terms and concepts with an identification of opportunities for you to illustrate the higher-level skills of analysis and evaluation. The scope for linking different topic areas is also shown. The topic areas are:

- Corporate aims and objectives
- Assessing changes in the business environment
- Managing change

In this section, key concepts are defined and each topic area ends with the following:

- Suggestions on how particular aspects could lend themselves to analysis. Ensure that you are confident in your understanding of these opportunities for analysis. Test and practise your understanding of the variety of ways in which a logical argument or line of reasoning can be developed.
- Opportunities for evaluation. Ensure you understand these and the arguments that might support such evaluation.
- A brief summary of links to other parts of the specification. These suggest how you might integrate your knowledge and understanding of different topic areas. Ensure that you understand how these areas are linked together.

The **Question and Answer** section provides a series of questions to help you practise your examination skills. The questions are split into essay-style questions on pre-issued themes such as those that will appear in Section A of the examination paper, followed by essay questions that are similar to those that appear in Section B. All questions are based on the format of the Unit 4 paper and are followed by two sample answers (an A-grade and a lower-grade response) interspersed by examiner's comments. The lower-grade answers demonstrate common errors and poor examination technique.

You should read the relevant topic areas in the Content Guidance section before attempting a question from the Question and Answer section, and only read the specimen answers after you have tackled the question yourself.

Integration

The AQA specification states that Unit 4 is synoptic and draws on all other units of the specification, including the AS units. Unit 4 considers the relationship between businesses and external factors, examines themes that are important in the strategic management of businesses (such as leadership and corporate culture), and considers how businesses can manage change successfully. The specification recommends that Unit 4 is studied through a variety of real business contexts to improve understanding of how the impact and response to change varies from business to business.

Content Guidance

Corporate aims and objectives

Understanding mission, aims and objectives

A **mission statement** is a qualitative statement of an organisation's aims. It uses language intended to motivate employees and convince customers, suppliers and those outside the firm of its sincerity and commitment. Some mission statements have been criticised for containing idealistic values that have no meaning in practice and are simply part of a public relations (PR) strategy to promote the company to the public.

Corporate aims are the long-term intentions of a business. They determine the way in which an organisation will develop, and provide a common purpose for everyone to identify with and work towards, and a collective view that helps to build team spirit and encourage commitment.

Corporate objectives are medium- to long-term targets that must be achieved in order to meet the stated aims of the business. They govern the targets for each division or department of the business; give a sense of direction to the whole organisation; act as a focus for decision making and effort and as a yardstick against which success or failure can be measured; and encourage a sense of common purpose among the workforce.

Key corporate aims and objectives can be concerned with any of the following:
- survival
- profit
- growth
- diversification
- market standing
- meeting the needs of other stakeholders

Other examples of corporate aims and objectives include:
- maximising shareholder wealth
- maximising sales revenue
- focusing on the firm's core capabilities rather than venturing into risky diversification
- social and environmental responsibility
- adding value
- enhancing reputation through continuous technological innovation

> **Examiner tip**
> Make sure you are confident in your knowledge of functional objectives and strategies relating to finance, marketing, operations and human resources, which you covered in Unit 3.

Long- and short-term corporate objectives may differ for a number of reasons:
- A financial crisis is likely to encourage a firm to focus on short-term survival rather than, say, growth or market share.
- A long-term objective of improving profitability may be sacrificed in the short term in order to try to eliminate a competitor.
- In a recession, the immediate emphasis is likely to be on survival.
- Changes in government policy may force a company to adopt different short-term priorities.
- Negative publicity from a faulty product or an environmental disaster will cause a firm to focus on improving its image in the short term.

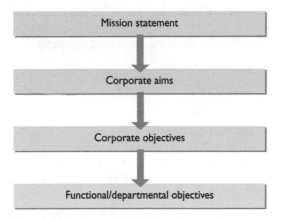

Figure 1 The hierarchy of objective setting within an organisation

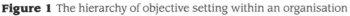

Corporate strategies are the general approaches a company will use and the policies and plans it develops in order to achieve its corporate aims and objectives.

Stakeholders are individuals or groups with a direct interest in the activities and performance of an organisation.

Common and conflicting aims or interests of stakeholders

A profitable and successful business is of common interest to all stakeholders. However, different stakeholder groups also have conflicting aims that may influence decision making in a business. The following list identifies the interests of the main stakeholder groups:
- **Shareholders** — high profit levels, a positive corporate image, long-term growth.
- **Employees** — job security, good working conditions, high levels of pay, promotional opportunities, job enrichment.
- **Customers** — high-quality products and services, low prices, good service, wide choice.
- **Suppliers** — regular/increasing orders, prompt payment, steady growth.
- **Local community** — employment opportunities, acting in a socially responsible manner.
- **Government** — efficient use of resources, employment and training, complying with legislation.

Knowledge check 1

Explain the reason for the hierarchy of objective setting as illustrated in Figure 1.

Knowledge check 2

Identify three internal and three external stakeholders.

Analysis

Opportunities for analysis include:

- examining the quality of a specific objective
- demonstrating the links between mission, aims and objectives
- considering the purpose and nature of corporate strategies
- analysing the relationship between corporate strategies and corporate aims and objectives
- considering the reasons for, and implications of, adopting short-term objectives
- identifying the common and conflicting aims of different stakeholder groups
- analysing how a business might prioritise the aims and interests of different stakeholder groups
- analysing the impact of the differing stakeholder perspectives on a company's decision making

Evaluation

Opportunities for evaluation include:

- evaluating the different influences on a firm's objectives
- discussing the merits and suitability of an organisation's objectives
- evaluating the relative merits of short- and long-term objectives in a particular situation
- judging the appropriateness of corporate strategies in relation to a firm's corporate objectives
- judging the degree of common and/or conflicting interests of different stakeholder groups
- discussing the differing stakeholder perspectives in a particular business context
- assessing the extent to which pressure from stakeholders affects business decision making

Links

Possible links to other areas include functional objectives and strategies in relation to finance, marketing, operations and human resources.

Summary

- For an organisation to achieve its stated aims, it must ensure that its activities and its staff are effectively coordinated and focused on meeting these aims.
- Broad corporate aims or goals are identified first. These are translated into more specific company-wide objectives. These are in turn translated into specific functional or departmental objectives for finance, marketing, operations and human resources.
- Stakeholders are those individuals and groups with a direct interest in the activities and performance of the organisation.
- Although a profitable and successful business is of common interest to all stakeholders, different stakeholder groups also have conflicting aims that may influence decision making in a business.
- An important responsibility for the business is to balance these conflicting aims and interests. In this context, limited resources and opportunity costs are fundamental issues to consider.

Assessing changes in the business environment

PESTLE analysis is a framework for assessing the likely impact of the political, economic, social, technological, legal and environmental factors on the external environment of a business. (This framework is also known as PEST analysis, with the legal element being included in the analysis of the political environment, and the environmental element in the social environment.)

Figure 2 The business and its environment

Examiner tip
When analysing a business, remember that it is vital to take into account the competitive and business environments in which it operates.

PESTLE analysis

PESTLE category	Examples of issues in each category that might affect business
Political factors	• extent of government intervention • government economic policies • membership of the EU
Economic factors	• the business cycle • economic growth • interest rates • exchange rates • level of inflation • level of unemployment • globalisation of markets • emerging markets
Social factors	• demographic factors • ethical issues • impact of pressure groups • influence of different stakeholders • changing lifestyles
Technological factors	• new products • new processes • impact of technological change • costs of technological change
Legal factors	Legislation related to: • employment • consumer protection • environmental protection • health and safety
Environmental factors	• costs of environmentally friendly policies • impact of environmentally friendly policies

The relationship between businesses and the economic environment

The business cycle

The **business cycle** is the regular pattern of increasing and decreasing demand and output within an economy or of growth in gross domestic product (GDP — the total value of a country's output over the course of a year) over time. It is characterised by four main phases: boom, recession (or downturn), slump (or depression) and recovery (or upturn).

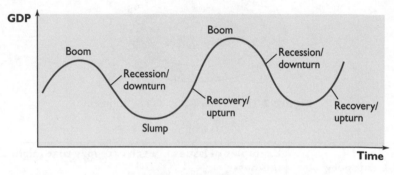

Figure 3 The business cycle

Possible causes of the business cycle

- Changes in business confidence, which lead to changes in the level of investment in fixed (non-current) assets.
- Periods of inventory building and then de-stocking.
- Irregular patterns of expenditure on consumer durables, such as cars, washing machines and televisions.
- Confidence in the banking sector and its ability to make sound decisions about who to lend money to.

Phases of the business cycle

Periods of **boom** are characterised by high levels of consumer demand, business confidence, profits, investment and business growth at the same time as rising costs, increasing prices and full capacity.

Periods of **recession** are characterised by falling levels of consumer demand, output, profit and business confidence, little investment, spare capacity, business closures and rising levels of unemployment.

Periods of **slump** are characterised by very low levels of consumer demand, investment and business confidence, an increasing number of businesses failing and high unemployment.

Knowledge check 3

Why might firms producing capital goods, such as machinery and plant, tend to suffer most in a recession?

Periods of **recovery** are characterised by slowly rising levels of consumer demand, rising investment, increasing business confidence, profits and business start-ups and falling levels of unemployment.

Business strategies in response to changes in the business cycle

The strategies a business might use will depend on which phase of the cycle the economy is in. For example, during a recession, many businesses will suffer declining demand. As a result they will wish to reduce production and improve efficiency. For many this will mean laying off workers in order to reduce costs and survive. Although this may be an appropriate strategy in the short term, in the longer term losing experienced staff could become problematic, especially when demand begins to improve and experienced workers are difficult to find.

Economic growth

Economic growth means an increase in the level of economic activity or GDP. It provides favourable trading conditions and new business opportunities. It offers more security and certainty to firms and therefore provides them with more confidence in planning for the future. However, economic growth can result in serious negative externalities, such as pollution, congestion and harm to the environment.

Business strategies in response to changes in the rate of economic growth

The effects of economic growth on business depend on whether the rate of economic growth is rapid, slowing down or actually decreasing, which reflects the various phases of the business cycle.

- **Impact on sales.** With higher levels of GDP, incomes in the economy are likely to be higher, which in turn is likely to lead to higher retail sales.
- **Impact on profits.** Higher incomes lead to greater demand for goods and services, which provides opportunities for firms to earn higher profits.
- **Impact on investment.** Higher demand for goods and services means that firms are more likely to invest in expanding their operations.
- **Impact on employment.** Once businesses are convinced that the increase in demand is sustainable, they are likely to want to recruit more workers.
- **Impact on business strategy.** The following business strategies are better suited to an environment of economic growth: expansion, new products and repositioning.

Interest rates

Interest rates are the cost of borrowing money and the return for lending money. They also measure the opportunity cost, to both individuals and firms, of spending money rather than saving it and receiving interest.

Implications of changes to the rate of interest

A fall in interest rates is likely to lead to:

Examiner tip

When analysing the impact of a particular phase of the business cycle on a firm, remember to consider the organisation and its products. For example, if a firm is producing and selling inferior goods, it may find that it benefits during a recession as incomes fall.

Knowledge check 4

What is meant by gross domestic product (GDP)?

Knowledge check 5

Explain the meaning of the term 'opportunity cost'.

- an increase in demand for consumer goods
- an increase in demand for capital goods
- a fall in costs and a rise in profits
- a fall in the exchange rate of the pound, which is likely to lead to a fall in export prices and a rise in import prices

If interest rates rise, the opposite effects will occur.

Business strategies in response to changes in interest rates

Strategies will depend on whether the rate of interest is rising or falling, the nature of the goods or services provided and what else is happening within the economy.

Strategies based on expansion tend to be used when interest rates are low.

Exchange rates

Exchange rates are the price of one country's currency in terms of another.

Implications for business of changes in exchange rates

The level of, and changes in, exchange rates affect businesses in different ways depending on whether they are:
- businesses that export their goods to other countries
- businesses that sell their goods in the UK, competing against foreign imports
- businesses that purchase imported fuel, raw materials and components to use in the production of their own goods

Assuming that profit margins remain the same, an increase in the exchange rate may increase the price at which exports are sold abroad and reduce the price charged for imports in the UK. This in turn will affect revenue, competitiveness and profitability. The extent to which the changing prices of exports and imports will affect export sales and the purchase of imports depends on the price elasticity of demand.

It is, however, important to note that the levels of export sales and import purchases are influenced not only by exchange rates, but also by a range of other factors, including reputation and quality, after-sales service, the reliability, design and desirability of the product, the overall packaging provided and payment terms.

Business strategies in response to changes in exchange rates

The strategies a business might deploy in response to changes in exchange rates will depend on whether exchange rates are rising or falling, what market the business operates in and whether it exports its goods to consumers in other countries, sells its goods in the UK in competition with foreign imports or purchases imported fuel, raw materials and components to use in the production of its own goods.

Inflation

Inflation is an increase in the general level of prices within an economy.

Effects of inflation on business

- If interest rates are less than the rate of inflation, borrowing is encouraged. For highly geared firms and those with heavy borrowing, inflation reduces the real value of the sum they owe, making it easier to repay the loan.
- As inflation rises, so too do property prices and the value of stock. Thus balance sheets tend to look healthier.
- Firms find it easier to increase their prices when inflation is present because cost increases can be passed on to the consumer more easily.
- Depending upon the price elasticity of demand for particular products, higher prices may mean lower sales.
- The producers of major brands that tend to sell at premium prices may suffer as inflation makes consumers more aware of the price differentials.
- As consumers become more aware of prices, workers become far more concerned about the level of their real wages because, unless they obtain a pay rise at least as high as the rate of inflation, their real income will fall.
- Suppliers may increase their prices, adding further to a firm's costs and putting more pressure on the firm to increase its own prices.
- If inflation in the UK is relatively higher than inflation in other countries, the international competitiveness of UK firms may be reduced.
- As the future is uncertain, forecasts of sales revenue and profits will become very difficult and planning will be less reliable.
- When prices are changing quickly, businesses find it more difficult to keep track of competitors' pricing strategies.
- Cash flow is squeezed as the costs of new materials and equipment rise.

Business strategies in response to inflation

When deciding how to respond to inflation, a business must consider whether inflation is low or high and what the nature of the business and the products or services it offers are. Strategies will also depend on what is happening to the prices of its supplies and the prices of its competitors' products both at home and abroad.

Unemployment

Unemployment is the number of jobless people who want to work, are available to work and are actively seeking employment.

Implications of high unemployment for business

- Consumer incomes fall, leading to lower sales.
- Workers have less bargaining power, meaning there is less pressure to increase wage levels.
- As demand falls, cost-saving strategies may be introduced.
- Lower demand is likely to lead to cutbacks or delays in investment projects.
- Lower demand and the need to reduce costs by reducing the workforce and investment may cause businesses to consider rationalisation as a strategy.

Examiner tip

Don't make the mistake of thinking that a fall in the inflation rate means a fall in prices. It simply means a slowing down of the rate at which prices are rising. Falling prices (or deflation) can only occur if the inflation rate is negative.

Knowledge check 8

Identify three adverse effects of inflation for a firm.

Knowledge check 9

State four main types of unemployment.

Knowledge check 10

What does the term 'rationalisation' mean? Give two examples of rationalisation that a firm might consider.

Business strategies in response to changes in the level of unemployment

Strategies will depend on the nature of the business and how efficient it is, and whether its products are normal, luxury or inferior.

The globalisation of markets and the development of emerging markets

Globalisation is the process of enabling financial and investment markets to operate internationally, largely as a result of deregulation and improved communications.

An **emerging market** is an international area that has the potential to grow and develop in terms of productive capacity, market opportunities and competitive advantage.

Analysis

Opportunities for analysis include:
- examining the impact of different macroeconomic variables on trading conditions for business in general or for a particular business
- analysing trends in key economic variables
- analysing the impact of different phases of the business cycle on business in general and on particular businesses
- considering how the different phases of the business cycle influence the demand for products with different price elasticities and those that are more or less sensitive to changes in income
- analysing how economic growth might affect a business organisation
- considering the disadvantages of economic growth and how these affect a firm's operations
- examining the implications of changes in interest rates on an organisation
- analysing the implications of changes in the exchange rate on a business
- considering price elasticity of demand when examining the effects of a strong/weak pound on exports and imports or the impact of inflation on business
- examining the effects of inflation on business
- considering how inflation influences business strategy
- analysing the implications of unemployment on a particular organisation
- analysing how a business can take advantage of globalisation
- analysing how a business can take advantage of emerging markets

Evaluation

Opportunities for evaluation include:
- assessing the impact of different economic factors on business organisations
- judging the relative impact of different macroeconomic variables on a business's short-term and long-term strategy
- assessing the extent to which a particular industry is affected by different phases of the business cycle

Knowledge check 11

Identify two reasons why a firm might wish to compete in international markets.

Knowledge check 12

Identify two possible benefits to UK firms of entering emerging markets such as those in eastern Europe.

- assessing the impact of economic growth on business organisations
- judging the extent to which economic growth benefits firms in different markets
- assessing the impact of changes in interest rates on business organisations
- evaluating how interest rate changes affect the sales of durable goods, such as cars and furniture, compared to smaller items that are not bought on credit
- assessing the impact of changes in exchange rates on business organisations
- evaluating the significance of exchange rate changes for a firm involved in exporting and for a firm involved in importing
- assessing the impact of inflation on business organisations
- assessing the impact of unemployment on business organisations
- evaluating the impact of globalisation, or of emerging markets, on the success of a particular business

Links

Possible links to other areas include pricing and elasticity of demand, budgeting, profitability, breakeven, investment appraisal, labour recruitment and remuneration — all of which are relevant to business strategies that might be introduced in response to changes in macroeconomic variables.

The relationship between businesses and the political and legal environment

Government intervention means policy based on the belief that government should exert a strong influence on the economy, rather than allowing market forces to dictate conditions. It includes the provision of products and services by government, economic policies such as monetary and fiscal policy, regulation and legislation.

Most governments in the developed world provide a range of what are considered to be essential products and services, including education, health and housing.

Government economic policies

Economic policy involves efforts by the government to control the economy in order to achieve its objectives of encouraging economic growth, controlling and reducing inflation, maintaining a satisfactory level of employment, achieving a satisfactory balance of payments and maintaining a stable exchange rate. The main economic policies are:

- **Monetary policy** — controlling the money supply and the rate of interest in order to influence the level of spending and demand in the economy.
- **Fiscal policy** — the use of taxation and government expenditure to influence the economy.
- **Supply-side policy** — measures taken to increase the UK's capacity to supply products in order to achieve growth.

Knowledge check 13

What is meant by the term 'market forces'?

Examiner tip

Ensure that you understand the possible implications of a change in interest rates, which were covered in the previous section.

Impact of monetary and fiscal policies on the economy and business

During a recession, growth can be encouraged by introducing measures that will increase demand. These include:

- Lowering interest rates to encourage investment and consumer spending.
- Cutting taxes to give people more spending power.
- Increasing government spending, which has multiplier effects throughout the economy. For example, the building of a new hospital involves the employment of builders and eventually of medical staff, all of who have incomes that they will spend in the local economy. Suppliers of raw materials will receive additional demand that may have favourable effects on their financial position, and so on.

The opposite measures might be used when the economy is booming, inflation is high and there are shortages of skilled labour.

Monetary and fiscal policies influence the overall level of demand in the economy. Supply-side policies aim to increase the efficiency of supply and how markets work. Most supply-side policies focus on particular parts of the economy rather than the economy as whole. Examples include: allowing the labour market to function efficiently by reducing the power of trade unions and improving incentives for people to find and retain jobs; raising the efficiency of business by improving access to education and training, increasing competition and reducing regulation.

Knowledge check 14

Explain how a rise in the rates of income tax, corporation tax and VAT might each affect businesses.

Political decisions affecting trade and access to markets

The enlargement of the European Union (EU)

From an original group of six countries in 1957, the EU expanded to 27 member states in 2007. The main features of the EU include:

- a customs union involving free trade between member states and a common external tariff barrier for products from non-EU countries
- common technical standards for EU products
- harmonised VAT and excise duties
- the free movement of people and capital within the EU
- a European Central Bank and a single European currency (the euro) adopted by 17 of the 27 countries of the EU

Implications of the enlarged EU for UK business

Implications of the enlarged EU for UK business include:

- access to a market of approximately 500 million people
- opportunities for economies of scale, lower costs and increased specialisation
- more competition, which may lead to improved efficiency, lower costs and more innovation
- greater mobility of labour, giving firms a wider labour force to draw on
- firms are able to set up anywhere in the EU, for example, where costs are lower
- increased legislation and the need to meet common technical standards

Knowledge check 15

What does the term 'economies of scale' mean?

Moves towards greater freedom of trade

The EU is an example of a free trade area, that is, a group of countries that agree to trade with each other without erecting any barriers to trade. This encourages competition between firms in the different member countries and, as a result, encourages greater efficiency in the delivery of goods and services and lower prices for consumers.

The World Trade Organization (WTO) is a group of 153 countries committed to the encouragement of fair international trade. It is a forum for the negotiation of trade agreements and the settling of trade disputes between countries. Its overriding purpose is to help 'trade flow as freely as possible'.

Impact of legislation relating to businesses

In general, legislation is intended to protect those with weaker bargaining power. It thus ensures a more ordered and predictable environment and one that is fairer for all parties concerned.

Employment legislation falls into two broad categories: individual employment law, which aims to ensure that employees and employers act fairly in dealing with each other; and collective labour law, which aims to control industrial relations and trade union activity.

Consumer protection legislation aims to safeguard consumers from exploitation or exposure to unsafe products or services.

Environmental protection legislation includes EU directives on a range of issues including air quality and the collection, transport, recovery and disposal of waste. Legislation in this area is also aimed at preventing or minimising pollution from emissions.

Health and safety legislation aims to provide a safe working environment for employees.

Implications of legislation for business

- Fewer working days are now lost because of strikes or industrial action.
- Additional costs might be incurred in order to comply with the legislation.
- Equal opportunities legislation is likely to ensure that the 'best' candidates are recruited.
- Motivation may improve if the relationship between employees and employers is clearly stated and understood by all parties and if safety and security in the work environment is of a high standard.
- A firm's reputation may improve as a result of complying with legislation: for example, the quality of its products improves; its sound environmental management helps to promote its products; or its good safety record has a beneficial effect on recruitment.
- Improved quality may lead to savings in relation to rejects and returns.

Knowledge check 16

The opposite of free trade is protectionism. State three types of protectionism.

Knowledge check 17

Explain one advantage to a business of each of the following:
- employment legislation
- consumer protection legislation
- environmental protection legislation
- health and safety legislation

Examiner tip

When considering the impact of specific areas of legislation, or legislation in general, try to weigh up the arguments — that is, *evaluate*. There will always be constraints and additional costs or administrative burdens imposed on a business in complying with legislation, but there will also be benefits for individual firms and consumers and for the wider business community.

Analysis

Opportunities for analysis include:

- analysing the impact of particular government economic policies on a business
- recognising how the impact of particular government economic policies will differ depending on the nature of the business and the nature of its products
- analysing the impact of an enlarged European Union on UK business
- considering how greater freedom of trade might benefit UK business
- considering how a business might adapt its strategies in order to respond to a change in legislation
- analysing the impact of particular areas of legislation on a business

Evaluation

Opportunities for evaluation include:

- assessing the extent to which particular businesses are influenced by different government economic policies
- evaluating the opportunities for a UK business of the enlargement of the EU
- discussing the impact of particular areas of legislation on particular organisations
- evaluating the responses of business to changes in the political and legal environment

Links

Possible links to other areas include changes in macroeconomic variables such as interest rates and their influence on business, marketing strategies, economies of scale and efficiency issues, location of industry, and elasticity of demand.

The relationship between businesses and the social environment

Changes in the social environment

Demographic factors include the characteristics of human populations and population groups, including elements such as age, ethnicity, gender, religion and sexual orientation. Demographic changes influence two important aspects of business — employees and customers. Depending on the nature of a business, demographic change can be either an opportunity or a threat.

Environmental issues include the externalities that a firm creates, i.e. the environmental effects of a firm's activities, which may be positive, such as job creation or providing a pleasing landscape around the factory, or negative, such as polluting the atmosphere with fumes or congesting the roads with lorries.

Examiner tip

A key issue in answering questions on this subject is to consider both costs and benefits. For example, a particular course of action may have environmental benefits but may also have negative externalities, such as unemployment.

Knowledge check 18

Define the term 'social costs' and give two examples.

Opportunities provided when a firm assumes environmental responsibility

- **Marketing opportunities.** A good reputation in relation to environmental issues can act as a positive marketing tool that encourages consumers to choose one brand over another.
- **Financial opportunities.** Firms may find it easier to gain finance if they are able to point to a solid record of helping rather than damaging the environment.
- **Human resource opportunities.** A reputation for protecting the environment can have positive effects on potential employees' perceptions of a firm.

The changing nature of the ethical environment

Business ethics are the moral principles that should underpin decision making. Ethical behaviour involves actions and decisions that are seen to be morally correct. Ethical dilemmas include:

- whether an advertising agency should accept a cigarette manufacturer as a client
- whether a firm should relocate to a country paying lower wages
- whether a firm should always pay suppliers on time or should delay as long as possible
- whether a manufacturer of military aircraft should sell to a foreign government suspected of using force to maintain power
- whether a firm should try to minimise its production costs and prices by using environmentally polluting processes

An **ethical code** is an instruction from an organisation to its employees to indicate how they should react to situations relating to moral values. **Ethical investment** refers to stock market investment based on a restricted list of firms that are seen as ethically sound.

Advantages of ethical behaviour

- Ethical behaviour can give companies a clear competitive advantage on which marketing activities can be based.
- Firms that adopt ethical practices may expect to recruit staff who are better qualified and motivated.

Problems with ethical positions

- An ethical choice can incur extra cost and thus reduce profits.
- People have different views about what is ethical and these views change over time.
- In large organisations, it may be difficult to inform staff of the ethical policy or ethical code and to monitor adherence to it.
- As empowered workers take more decisions, it becomes harder to maintain a consistent company policy on ethical behaviour.

Corporate social responsibility (CSR) involves the duties of an organisation towards employees, customers, society and the environment. Examples of activities that would be viewed as socially responsible include:

Examiner tip
Business ethics is an important element of the specification and is an area where you are usually required to demonstrate the skill of evaluation. Ensure that you provide well-argued points in your answers to questions about ethics and avoid the temptation to make value judgements and assertions that are unsupported by argument or evidence.

Examiner tip
Don't confuse ethical behaviour with behaviour that is within the law. Behaving in an ethical way is more than behaving according to the law.

- using sustainable sources of raw materials
- ensuring that suppliers operate responsibly — for example, not using child labour
- operating an extensive health and safety policy above the legal requirements, thereby protecting the wellbeing of employees
- engaging in a continuous process of environmental management and monitoring the effects of production on the environment
- trading ethically and taking account of moral issues

Analysis

Opportunities for analysis include:

- considering the pressures and opportunities that arise from environmental issues
- examining the influence of business ethics on a firm's decision-making processes
- demonstrating the consequences of a particular ethical or socially influenced decision
- analysing the conflict between profit and ethics
- analysing the pros and cons of a firm accepting its social responsibilities
- examining the level of social responsibility shown by a firm
- showing how a more socially responsible (or ethical) policy can be implemented
- analysing why a firm might want to become more (or less) socially responsible

Evaluation

Opportunities for evaluation include:

- judging the extent to which a firm should, and is able to, take responsibility for environmental issues
- evaluating the extent to which social and ethical decisions depend on other factors such as the market and competition
- discussing the potential conflict that could occur between business ethics and business efficiency
- assessing whether a firm should accept its social responsibilities

Links

Possible links to other areas include human resource management, marketing, costing and business efficiency.

The relationship between businesses and the technological environment

The technological environment

Technological change means adapting new applications of practical or mechanical sciences to industry and commerce.

Information technology is the creation, storage and communication of information using microelectronics, computers and telecommunications.

Benefits of technological change

Benefits include:

- improved efficiency and reduced waste
- better products and services
- new products and materials
- advances in communication
- improved working environment
- higher living standards

Issues to consider when introducing new technology

Issues to consider include:

- knowing what new technology to buy and when to buy it, and ensuring that new technology is compatible with existing technology
- the reaction of the workforce, whose cooperation is essential, especially when technology is replacing jobs or changing the nature of jobs
- the new skills required and the implications for recruitment, retention and training and their associated costs
- short-term difficulties, such as possible cutbacks in production
- the cost of keeping up to date with the latest technology and the huge financial costs in the short term
- marketing opportunities
- the culture of the business
- the processes and systems used within the business

Analysis

Opportunities for analysis include:

- analysing the benefits and problems associated with technological change
- examining the impact of technological change in relation to the marketing opportunities open to a business, the culture of a business and the processes and systems used within a business
- considering the responses of a particular business to technological change

Evaluation

Opportunities for evaluation include:

- evaluating the extent to which the benefits of new technology outweigh the problems created by new technology
- discussing the impact of technological change on different elements of a business
- assessing the response of a particular business to technological change

Examiner tip

Remember that the issues considered in this section should be viewed as part of the external environment of a business. When analysing or evaluating the external environment facing a business, ensure that you make use of the PESTLE framework. This will encourage you to think about other aspects of the external environment, not just the technological environment.

Knowledge check 19

Identify an example of technological change in each of the primary, secondary and tertiary sectors of industry.

Examiner tip

The impact and effect of technological change is viewed differently by different stakeholders, so remember when answering evaluative questions about this area to be aware of the arguments from differing points of view. Read the question carefully to make sure that you are answering it relevantly — for example, it may want a specific stakeholder's view.

Links

Possible links to other areas include investment appraisal to determine the financial viability of introducing a particular type of technological change; elements of marketing and the marketing opportunities that emerge as a result of technological change; corporate culture and its impact on, and how it is affected by, technological change; and elements of operations management and how this is affected by the introduction of technological change.

The relationship between businesses and the competitive environment

The competitive structure

Some businesses operate in very competitive markets, where there are many small firms, each selling only a very small proportion of the total market sales. Other businesses operate in markets that tend to be dominated by a few large firms, each selling a significant proportion of the total market sales.

Examiner tip
The characteristics of the main types of market structures in which firms operate were covered in Units 2 and 3, so ensure that you are familiar with them before proceeding.

Changes in competitive structure

The emergence of new competitors

This can occur because a new business enters the industry. In order to compete, existing businesses will need to ensure that their products or services are of an appropriate quality, are priced and promoted appropriately and have their own USPs. In some industries, barriers to entry prevent or deter new firms from entering.

Barriers to entry include:

- the high capital costs required to set up a new business
- patents that allow existing firms to 'monopolise' the market legally
- the loyalty of customers to existing firms
- the need to achieve large economies of scale quickly in order to be able to charge a competitive price
- government policy and regulation
- access to resources and distribution channels

The development of dominant businesses

From being a relatively small player in a market, a business can develop into a dominant business as a result of a takeover or a merger.

Changes in the buying power of customers

The power of customers is related to their ability to influence the price that they pay. The extent to which an individual customer has power over a business will depend on whether they are one among many customers or one of only a small number of customers.

Changes in the selling power of suppliers

The power of suppliers is related to their ability to influence the prices they will receive for their supplies. The more concentrated and controlled the source of supply, the more power the supplier is likely to wield in the market. This will be determined by whether the resources a business requires are purchased from a small firm for which there are many alternative competing suppliers or from a large firm that is the only source of the supply.

Responses to changes in the competitive environment

If a new competitor emerges in the market, a business might try to diversify into other markets or consider merging with or taking over another business in order to establish itself as a dominant business in the market.

If a supplier has too much power over a business, one possibility is for the business to find alternative sources of supply.

If a business currently sells to a single buyer, its strategy might be to find more buyers in order to reduce the power of any one buyer.

Analysis

Opportunities for analysis include:
- considering the effects of changes in the competitive structure of an industry on a particular business
- examining the type of responses a business might make to the changing competitive environment

Evaluation

Opportunities for evaluation include:
- assessing the effects of changes in the competitive structure faced by a business
- evaluating the responses of a business to a changing competitive environment

Links

Possible links to other areas are market structures, including monopoly, oligopoly, monopolistic competition and perfect competition, and Porter's five competitive forces.

Examiner tip

Michael Porter's idea of competitive forces identified the features of markets that determine how a successful firm might cope with its competitors. This was covered at AS, so review this before proceeding.

Knowledge check 20

Distinguish between fair and unfair competition.

Examiner tip

Remember that the competitive environment does not just refer to the home or domestic market; it includes the international competitive environment in which business operates.

Summary

- PEST or PESTLE analysis provides a framework for assessing the likely impact of the political, economic, social, technological, legal and environmental factors in the external environment of a business.

- Key macroeconomic variables that affect businesses include: the business cycle, economic growth, interest rates, exchange rates, inflation and unemployment. Businesses use a range of strategies to take advantage of the opportunities that changes in these variables create or to reduce the adverse impact of such changes.

- Businesses must also ensure that they have strategies in place either to take advantage of opportunities provided by globalisation and emerging markets or to reduce the adverse impact of such developments.

- Government intervention involves the provision of products by the government, government regulation and legislation and other forms of intervention such as tax and subsidy.

- Government economic policies include monetary policy, fiscal policy and supply-side policies.

- Political decisions affecting trade and access to markets include the enlargement of the European Union and moves towards greater freedom of trade.

- Legislation affecting business includes that relating to employment, consumer protection, environmental protection and health and safety.

- The social environment includes demographic and environmental issues and the changing nature of the ethical environment a business is faced with.

- Business responses to the changing social environment can be seen in the actions they take to demonstrate corporate social responsibility. An important element of this is to evaluate the extent to which actions in relation to corporate social responsibility reflect genuine values or are just a form of public relations.

- The impact of technological change is particularly evident in relation to marketing opportunities, business culture and the processes and systems used within business.

- The competitive structure in which a business operates and how effectively it responds to changes to this competitive structure will have a major impact on its success.

- Changes in competitive structure include the emergence of new competitors, the development of dominant businesses (for example, through takeover or merger) and changes in the buying power of customers and/or the selling power of suppliers.

Managing change

Internal causes of change

Change in organisational size

Examiner tip
Synergy, which means that the whole is greater than the sum of the parts (1 + 1 = 3), is often claimed to be a major advantage of takeovers. The evidence suggests that it is achieved less often than is claimed.

Internal or organic growth is when a firm expands its existing capacity or range of activities by extending its premises or building new factories from its own resources, rather than by integration with another firm.

External growth comes about by the integration of two or more businesses via a merger or takeover.

A **merger** is where two or more firms agree to come together under one board of directors. A **takeover** (or acquisition) is where one firm buys a majority shareholding in another firm and therefore assumes full management control.

External growth is usually the fastest way to achieve growth, but, given the problems of integrating two separate organisations, can also be risky. External growth, whether by merger or takeover, can be classified into three broad types of integration: vertical, horizontal and conglomerate.

Vertical integration is the coming together of firms in the same industry but at different stages of the production process. It includes backward and forward integration. Vertical integration:
- enables internal planning and coordination of processes to overcome the uncertainty of dealing with external suppliers and retailers
- facilitates cost savings in both technical and marketing areas
- builds barriers to entry for new competitors
- enables the resulting organisation to absorb the profit margins of suppliers and/ or retailers

Horizontal integration is the coming together of firms operating at the same stage of production and in the same market. Firms involved in horizontal integration are usually potential competitors. Horizontal integration results in:
- economies of scale
- lower unit costs
- reduced competition
- increased market share

Conglomerate integration is the coming together of firms operating in unrelated markets. Conglomerate integration results in:
- the spreading of risks through diversification
- the sharing of good practice between different areas of the business

However, management may have little or no expertise in the newly acquired business area.

Retrenchment means the cutting back of an organisation's scale of operations. It can take a range of forms, including:
- halting recruitment or offering early retirement or voluntary redundancy
- delayering
- closing a factory, outlet or division of the business
- making targeted cutbacks and redundancies throughout the business

New owners/leaders

Managing growth

Growth often means that owners, who have been in complete control of all aspects of a business, have to plan for, and then adjust to, handing over responsibility to others. In comparison to leaders of a medium-sized business, the leaders in a large business tend to have a much less hands-on approach and need to delegate much more. Equally, in a large business, the task of controlling and coordinating activities is much more difficult.

Without strong and effective management, growth can result in a loss of direction and control. The demands placed on a leader/manager in relation to managing and

Knowledge check 21

Explain the term 'delayering'.

motivating a large team require very different skills from those needed in a medium-sized business. Introducing a solid organisational structure, having an effective management team and carrying out detailed financial and operational planning and forecasting are vital.

Bringing in a management team

As a business grows it will need restructuring. In most instances, the expertise to build and manage that structure will come from outside the business. A bigger company needs managers to take control of departments and a hierarchy that includes people with the expertise and the time to drive it forward.

Private investors and venture capital firms evaluate management structures and expertise before committing funding, and often insist on recruiting new or interim management. This can be seen as a way of taking control away from the founder, but it is often a means of protecting the investment by ensuring that any skills gaps are plugged and that the necessary structures and experience are in place.

Poor business performance

Internal change can also come about as a result of the poor performance of a business. Such a situation may lead to a change in the size of the business, a change in ownership or changes in leaders and senior managers.

Analysis

Opportunities for analysis include:
- analysing the implications for a firm of organic growth as compared with external growth
- examining the motives for the various types of external growth available to a firm
- analysing the effect of different types of retrenchment on a business and on its stakeholders
- examining the difference between the role of owner/boss and owner/manager as a business grows
- considering the reluctance of owners/managers to delegate as a business grows and examining the problems that this might cause
- considering how poor business performance might lead to internal change in a business

Evaluation

Opportunities for evaluation include:
- judging whether internal or external growth is the most appropriate means for a particular business
- evaluating the arguments for and against each type of external growth for a particular organisation
- judging the type of retrenchment that is likely to have the least adverse effects on the workforce or on particular stakeholder groups

- assessing the issues to consider in leading and managing a growing business
- evaluating the extent to which new owners/leaders benefit a business as it grows
- assessing how poor business performance might lead to a decline in the size of a business

Links

Possible links to other areas include the legal structure of business, organisational structure, delegation, motivation, leadership, and financial, marketing, operations management and human resource issues linked to business growth.

Planning for change

The purpose and value of corporate plans

Corporate plans are strategies detailing how a firm's aims and objectives will be achieved. They comprise medium- and long-term actions.

A corporate plan:
- clarifies the role of each department in contributing to meeting the aims and objectives of the organisation
- allows for better coordination of activities within a business
- helps to identify the resources required by the organisation and so makes it easier to raise finance by providing a clear plan of action, indicating how and why investment is required

Its success depends on a number of issues, including:
- whether it is the right plan for the business in its present circumstances
- whether there are adequate financial, human or production resources to implement the plan
- the probable actions and reactions of competitors
- how changes in the external environment are likely to affect the plan and the business

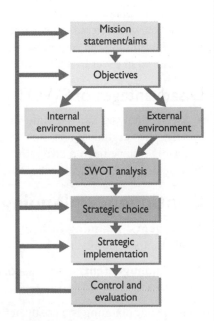

Figure 4 Map of the corporate planning process

Assessing internal and external influences on corporate plans: SWOT analysis

SWOT analysis is a technique that allows an organisation to assess its overall position, or the position of one of its divisions, products or activities. The internal audit of the company represents the present position of the product or company (its strengths and weaknesses), whereas the external audit represents the future potential of the company (its opportunities and threats).

An **internal audit** is an assessment of the strengths and weaknesses of a firm in relation to its competitors. It involves looking at current resources, how well they are managed and how well they match up to the demands of the market and to competition. It needs to range across all aspects of each of the functional areas.

An **external audit** is an assessment of the opportunities and threats facing a firm in the general business environment, i.e. the factors that have the potential to benefit the organisation and the factors that have the potential to cause problems for the organisation. It involves looking at the possibilities for development in different directions in the future. One method of analysing these external factors is to categorise them according to a PESTLE analysis (see page 9).

Advantages of SWOT analysis

- It highlights current and potential changes in the market and encourages an outward-looking approach.
- It encourages firms to develop and build upon existing strengths.
- It relates the present position and future potential of a business to the market in which it operates and the competitive forces within it, and is thus an excellent basis on which to make decisions.
- By determining the organisation's position, it influences the strategy that will be employed in order to achieve the organisation's aims and objectives.

Disadvantages of SWOT analysis

A SWOT analysis can be time consuming and the external factors can change rapidly. Thus organisations must use the results of a SWOT analysis with caution — what might have been a strength in the past may now be a weakness or what was previously a threat may now be an opportunity.

Contingency planning

Contingency planning means preparing for unexpected and usually unwelcome events that are, however, reasonably predictable and quantifiable.

Crisis management means responding to a sudden event that poses a significant threat to a firm.

Contingency planning is a costly activity. In large firms, it can involve huge numbers of highly qualified staff in assessing risk and planning what to do if things go wrong. Like any other form of insurance, it reduces risk but may seem like a waste of money if nothing ultimately goes wrong.

Knowledge check 24

Using a business with which you are familiar, provide one example of each of the following: a strength, a weakness, an opportunity and a threat.

Knowledge check 25

Identify the stages involved in contingency planning.

Examiner tip

An important aspect of responding promptly to a crisis is to ensure that all functional areas are working together.

Analysis

Opportunities for analysis include:

- considering the purpose and value of corporate plans for businesses
- analysing the various internal and external influences on the corporate plans of a business
- examining the differences between contingency planning and crisis management

Evaluation

Opportunities for evaluation include:

- assessing the extent to which a corporate plan helps a firm to pursue its objectives
- evaluating the relative importance for a business of the internal and external influences it faces and how these influence its corporate plans
- discussing to what extent a firm should deal differently with a real crisis compared to a fairly predictable and quantifiable risk
- judging how well contingency planning enables a firm to deal with the unexpected

Links

Possible links to other areas include elements of marketing, accounting and finance, people, operations management, and external influences.

Key influences on the change process: leadership

Leadership means deciding on a direction for a company in relation to its objectives and inspiring staff to achieve those objectives.

Management means getting things done by organising other people to do it.

Leadership styles

- **Authoritarian leadership** — a Taylorite style of leadership in which communication tends to be one-way: top-down.
- **Paternalistic leadership** — a leadership style in which employees are consulted but decision making remains firmly at the top.
- **Democratic leadership** — a leadership style involving two-way communication and considerable delegation.
- **Laissez-faire leadership** — a leadership style that abdicates responsibility and essentially takes a 'hands-off' approach.

Knowledge check 26

Provide two reasons why leadership style might be such an important element of business success.

McGregor's Theory X and Theory Y

A Theory X manager assumes that workers:
- are lazy, dislike work and are motivated by money
- need to be supervised and controlled or they will underperform
- have no wish or ability to help make decisions or take on responsibility
- are not interested in the needs of the organisation and lack ambition

A Theory Y manager assumes that:
- workers have many different needs, enjoy work and seek satisfaction from it
- workers will organise themselves and take responsibility to do so
- poor performance is likely to be due to monotonous work or poor management
- workers wish to, and should, contribute to decisions

Internal and external factors influencing leadership style

Figure 5 identifies a broad range of influences on leadership style. Most of these are internal factors, although 'The particular situation' could include external factors, such as the influence of the competitive market in which the business operates or whether a rival firm is attempting a takeover.

Figure 5 Influences on the choice of leadership style

The culture of an organisation affects, and is affected by, the style of leadership, which in turn is a major influence on the degree and effectiveness of delegation and consultation. The culture of an organisation will also affect the amount of resistance to change and therefore the ability of new leaders to impose their style or decisions on subordinates.

The role of leadership in managing change

Successful management of change requires effective leadership in order to ensure that changes to business strategy and operations are effectively anticipated, organised, introduced and evaluated.

Knowledge check 27

What is meant by the term 'change management'?

Analysis

Opportunities for analysis include:
- analysing the difference between the roles of leaders and managers
- considering the range of leadership styles
- examining internal and external factors influencing leadership style
- considering the role of leadership in managing change

Evaluation

Opportunities for evaluation include:
- discussing the difference between the roles of leaders and managers
- evaluating how different leadership styles are likely to benefit business
- assessing internal and external factors influencing leadership style
- discussing the role of leadership in managing change
- assessing the importance of leadership

Links

Possible links to other areas include culture, delegation, consultation and motivation.

Key influences on the change process: culture

Types of organisational culture

Organisational culture is the unwritten code that affects the attitudes and behaviour of staff, approaches to decision making and the leadership style of management.

Charles Handy's classification system

- **Power culture.** This is where a powerful individual or small group determines the dominant culture. Power culture is like a web with a ruling spider. Those in the web are dependent on a central power source. Rays of power and influence spread out from the central figure or group.
- **Role culture.** An organisation with a role culture is often referred to as a bureaucracy. Such organisations are controlled by procedures and role descriptions. Coordination is from the top and job positions are central. Such organisations value predictability and consistency, and may find it hard to adjust to change.

Examiner tip
Culture is often described as 'the way that we do things around here', meaning the type of behaviour that is considered acceptable or unacceptable, and is a result of tradition, history and structure.

Examiner tip
Corporate culture, change management and the differing approaches of small and large organisations are important concepts to consider when answering questions on management structure and organisation.

- **Task culture.** This is where the organisation's values are related to a job or project. Task culture is usually evident in small teams or organisations cooperating to deliver a project. The emphasis is on results and getting things done. Individuals are empowered with independence and control over their work.
- **Person culture.** This culture occurs in universities and in professions, such as accountancy and legal firms, where the organisation exists as a vehicle for people to develop their own careers and expertise. The individual is the central point. If there is a structure, it exists only to serve the individuals within it.

Bureaucratic and entrepreneurial cultures

Bureaucratic cultures have the following characteristics:

- an emphasis on roles and procedures (rather like Handy's role culture)
- risk averse and anxious to avoid mistakes
- generalised and non-commercial goals
- precisely defined responsibilities and roles
- a hierarchical structure

Entrepreneurial cultures have the following characteristics:

- an emphasis on results and rewards for individual initiative (rather like Handy's power culture)
- risk taking
- quantitative and financial goals
- a task culture with flexible roles
- a flatter and more flexible structure, giving more local control

Changing organisational culture

Organisational culture may change as a result of:
- a change in the external environment
- a merger or takeover
- a change in leadership

Changing organisational culture may involve the following problems:

- existing organisational culture, which when challenged may produce strong resistance
- leaders and senior managers, who may not communicate the case for cultural change effectively
- inadequate training, which may not prepare employees effectively for cultural change
- inappropriate recruitment, which may lead to the wrong people being employed
- inappropriate organisational structure, which may constrain entrepreneurial flair and risk taking

The importance of organisational culture

- It determines how firms respond to changes in their external environment.
- It has an important bearing on an organisation's behaviour and performance.
- It influences organisational structure (as well as being influenced by it).
- It is influential in the development of mission statements.

Examiner tip

In studying the culture of an organisation, focus not on what the organisation says, but on what it does.

Knowledge check 28

For each of the following types of organisations, explain their key feature and provide a real business example to illustrate: marketing-orientated organisations; production-orientated organisations; technology-orientated organisations.

- It affects leadership styles and has a major effect on the degree and effectiveness of delegation and consultation.
- It affects how well a business is able to introduce change.
- It influences the success of a business.

Analysis

Opportunities for analysis include:
- considering the different types of organisational culture and how these might influence an organisation's decision making
- analysing the reasons for, and the problems of, changing organisational culture

Evaluation

Opportunities for evaluation include:
- discussing to what extent the culture of an organisation might impede its ability to change in the future
- assessing the difficulties of changing organisational culture
- evaluating the extent to which an organisation's culture might influence its decision making
- assessing the importance of organisational culture

Links

Possible links to other areas include corporate aims and objectives, conflicting and common goals of stakeholders, organisational structures, leadership, mergers and takeovers.

Making strategic decisions

The significance of information management

Information management is the application of management techniques to collect information, communicate it within and outside the organisation, and process it to enable managers to make better decisions more quickly.

Effective information management is valuable because:
- it improves the ability to process information and make decisions
- as a result of sophisticated computerised systems, it is a powerful resource

The limitations of information management systems include:
- cost and time involved — it is not always possible or desirable (in terms of time, effort and cost) to access, collect and evaluate every piece of information or evidence that is relevant for taking a certain decision
- established organisational rules and procedures, organisational culture and the attitudes of leadership might prevent the optimal, or best, decision being taken

Different approaches to decision making and their value

Scientific decision making means taking a logical and research-based approach to decision making.

Knowledge check 29

Identify three quantitative decision-making techniques that might be employed to analyse data when using the scientific approach to decision making.

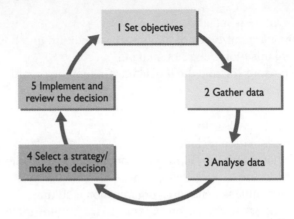

Figure 6 Scientific decision-making model

Benefits of using a scientific approach to decision making:
- it provides a clear sense of direction
- decisions are based on comparisons between alternative approaches
- it is likely that more than one person will be involved in the process
- decisions are monitored continually and reviewed
- the approach is flexible and the process can be reviewed and changed
- if all decisions are based on rational thinking, overall success is more probable
- it is easier to defend a policy developed on the basis of good planning

Hunch, or an **intuitive approach** to decision making, means decisions being made on the basis of a gut feeling or the personal views of the manager. Few decisions can be made on a purely objective basis; most include a subjective element based on managerial experience and intuition. Thus the benefits of using hunches are, in general, the problems of a scientific approach, which include:
- a scientific approach is a very expensive process
- a scientific approach is time consuming
- data collected in a scientific approach to decision making might be flawed
- invariably, scientific decisions are based on past information

The following factors are critical in deciding which approach to use:
- the speed at which a decision needs to be made
- the information available
- the size of the business
- the predictability of the situation
- the character of the person or the culture of the company

Other decision-making approaches include decision trees, Ansoff's matrix and Porter's generic strategies, which were considered in Unit 3.

Influences on corporate decision making

Ethical positions

A business may adopt a seemingly ethical position that is popular with consumers and is likely to lead to increased sales. Whether this is a reflection of the business adopting a 'real' ethical position or a 'perceived' one (i.e. as a PR exercise in order to gain consumer loyalty and increase sales) is debatable.

Resources

The resources available to a business, whether financial, human or physical, have a huge influence on corporate plans and corporate decisions.

The relative power of the stakeholders

The relative power and influence of stakeholder groups on decision making depends on the nature of the business. For example:

- in small family businesses, the interests of shareholders may be the major influence on decision making
- for organisations whose location has a major impact on the local environment, local communities or environmental pressure groups may be influential
- for businesses in highly competitive markets, the needs of customers will be a major influence on decision making
- employees will be powerful stakeholders in businesses that are dependent on a highly skilled but hard to find workforce

Analysis

Opportunities for analysis include:
- considering the significance of information management
- analysing how different approaches to decision making influence business success
- examining the influences on corporate decision making

Evaluation

Opportunities for evaluation include:
- assessing the significance of information management to business
- judging the extent to which intuitive and scientific approaches to decision making influence business success
- evaluating the influences on corporate decision making

Links

Possible links include marketing strategy, objectives and strategy in relation to methods of growth (horizontal, vertical and conglomerate), operations management in relation to research and development, and opportunity cost.

Knowledge check 30

Distinguish between a stakeholder and a shareholder.

Implementing and managing change

Techniques to implement and manage change

Project champions, project management and project groups

A **project champion** has two essential roles in relation to a project:
- to advocate and promote the benefits of pursuing the project
- to overcome funding constraints or problems with resource allocation

Desirable characteristics of a project champion include:
- involvement in the organisation's decision-making process
- a commitment to pursuing support for the project within the organisation
- good people skills and the ability to build relationships easily

Good **project management** means that things get done on time, within budget and meet or exceed the expectations of the business.

Project groups provide opportunities for job enlargement (as workers are often allowed to take on a variety of different tasks within the group) and synergy (because the combined results of the project group working together as a team of individuals is greater than the individual parts).

External consultants and external specialists

External consultants and specialists are often brought in when an organisation does not have the expertise itself or where its management needs to remain focused on existing business.

Factors that promote or resist change

Key factors that promote or resist change are:
- the clarity of objectives
- the appropriateness and sufficiency of resources
- the appropriateness of training

For example, to introduce a new IT system successfully there should be SMART objectives to justify its introduction, sufficient resources to ensure its success and training to ensure staff have the appropriate skills.

Other factors include:
- the degree of resistance to change
- the effectiveness of planning
- the impact on employees and how the business deals with this
- the skills and commitment of employees
- the effectiveness of teams
- the nature of the organisational structure
- external factors

Examiner tip

Remember — a project champion is not a formal project team member, but is someone who believes strongly in the project's goals and value.

Knowledge check 31

Explain the difference between a project manager and a project champion.

Examiner tip

Although it is generally agreed that effective change management is best driven by people in the organisation undergoing the change, they may be supported, where necessary, by external specialists. For example, a change manager with a track record of delivering successful change in similar circumstances may be brought in as an additional, temporary member of the team.

Knowledge check 32

What type of organisational structure is likely to facilitate change most successfully?

Knowledge check 33

Identify two external factors that might promote or cause resistance to change.

Analysis

Opportunities for analysis include:
- examining the techniques available for implementing and managing change successfully
- analysing the factors that promote change and those that resist change

Evaluation

Opportunities for evaluation include:
- evaluating the effectiveness of techniques used by a particular business to implement and manage change successfully
- assessing the factors that promote change and those that resist change in a particular business context

Links

Possible links include matrix management, leadership, teamwork and motivation.

Summary

- As well as external factors causing businesses to change their strategies, internal factors such as new owners and leaders, poor business performance and changes in organisational size, also lead to change. Changes in organisational size may come about because of mergers, takeovers, organic growth or retrenchment.

- Planning for change involves the creation of corporate plans. Internal and external influences affect these plans. Businesses also need to be alert to the unexpected by including contingency planning as part of their corporate planning.

- Leadership is an important influence in managing change. The roles of leaders differ from those of managers. A range of leadership styles exist, including authoritarian, paternalistic, democratic and laissez-faire. Internal and external factors influence leadership style.

- The culture of an organisation is an important influence on the change process. Different types of organisational cultures exist, including power, entrepreneurial and task-based cultures. Cultural change may be intended or unintended and may be the result of a number of different factors, including changes in the external environment or in leadership.

- Strategic decision making can take an intuitive or a scientific approach. Each approach has its benefits. Influences on corporate decision making include whether to adopt an ethical position (real or perceived), the resources available and the relative power of stakeholders.

- Techniques to implement and manage change successfully include project champions and project groups. A range of different factors promote and resist change, including the clarity of objectives, the availability of resources and the effectiveness of training.

Questions & Answers

This section of the guide is in two parts: Section A and Section B.

- Section A consists of four Unit 4-style pre-issued research themes, each of which includes associated stimulus material, one 40-mark question and two sample answers, including examiner comments and grade judgements.
- Section B provides four 40-mark essay questions, with two sample answers for each, including examiner comments and grade judgements.

Questions

The questions are based on the format of the AQA A2 Unit 4 papers.

For practice, you are advised to select one pre-issued research theme to explore. You should avoid reading the additional stimulus material or associated question at this stage. Once research has been carried out, you should sit a simulated examination by reading the additional stimulus material for the research theme and answering the associated question and then selecting one of the essay questions to answer. Allow yourself 1 hour 45 minutes to answer a research theme question and an essay question.

For additional practice, tackle the remaining questions in this book to develop your examination technique. To avoid overlap in the sample student answers, only one question is provided for each pre-issued theme. In the actual examination, you have to answer one question from a choice of two.

Remember, you will be given credit for using business concepts from outside this unit, as long as their inclusion and use is relevant to the question. This is particularly important in Unit 4, which is the synoptic unit, meaning it draws on your knowledge from all four units of the A-level assessment.

Sample answers

Resist the temptation to study the answers before you have attempted the questions. In each case, the first answer (by student A) is intended to show the type of response that would earn an A grade for that question. An A grade does not mean perfection — these answers show the range of responses that can earn high marks. In business studies, it is the quality of the reasoning that is rewarded. The quality of student B's answers varies from a U grade to an E grade; these answers contain examples of inappropriate approaches and common mistakes.

Examiner's comments

The examiner's comments indicate where credit is due. In the weaker answers, the comments point out areas for improvement, specific problems and common errors.

Assessment

A-level papers are designed to test certain skills. Every mark that is awarded on an A-level paper is given for the demonstration of a skill. The content of the course (the theories, concepts and ideas) provides a framework to allow students to show their skills. Recognising the content on its own is not enough to merit high marks.

The following skills are tested:
- **Knowledge and understanding** — recognising and describing business concepts and ideas.
- **Application** — being able to explain or apply your understanding.
- **Analysis** — developing a line of thought in order to demonstrate its impact or consequences.
- **Evaluation** — making a judgement by weighing up the evidence provided.

Unit 4 assessment

Unit 4 is assessed by an examination with a time allocation of 1 hour 45 minutes, which is worth 80 marks. All questions are essay-style. The examination consists of two sections:
- Section A is a pre-issued research task, which, together with additional brief stimulus material provided at the time of the examination, forms the basis of two essay-style questions, worth 40 marks each. Candidates must answer one question only.
- Section B consists of three essay questions, worth 40 marks each. Candidates must answer one question only.

All Unit 4 questions are evaluative, essay-style and synoptic. A synoptic question requires the integration of knowledge, understanding and skills learnt in different parts of the A-level course. This means that it assesses your understanding of the relationship between the different aspects of business studies, and requires you to use knowledge and skills acquired throughout the course.

The weighting of the four assessment objectives, in total and for each individual question, is as follows:

Unit 4 assessment objectives	Weighting
Knowledge: how well you know business theories, concepts and ideas	20%
Application: how well you can apply your knowledge and understanding to particular business contexts	20%
Analysis: how well you develop ideas, apply theory, consider implications and link issues; how well you develop a line of thought in order to demonstrate its impact or consequences	20%
Evaluation: how well you make a judgement by weighing up the evidence provided; how well you judge the overall significance of a situation	40%

Note: the skill of evaluation has greater weight in Unit 4 than in Unit 3, forming 40% of the total marks. Bear this in mind during your preparation and revision, as you will need to practise the skill of evaluation when writing your answers.

As all questions in Unit 4 require you to evaluate, all the trigger or key words used in the questions will be those that ask you to evaluate. Examples include:

- 'Assess...'
- 'Discuss...'
- 'To what extent...?'
- 'Evaluate...'
- 'Provide a reasoned judgement...'

When answering evaluative questions, remember that evaluation must be based on sound analysis, which in turn should be based on sound logic and/or the integration of business theory or concepts into an argument. Try to ensure that you provide a detailed conclusion and that you demonstrate judgement in weighing up the relative importance of different arguments. Although application has a lower weighting (20%), it is still an essential skill. The quality of a judgement invariably relies on the context of the question, and so your ability to apply your conclusion to the context of the question or theme will help you to earn application and evaluation marks.

Guidance on essay and essay-style questions

The following points provide guidance on how to answer essay and essay-style questions.

- An essay is a response to a specific question. The question is usually worded so that it cannot be answered by repeating paragraphs from notes. Hence, there is no such thing as the 'economic factors' essay or the 'leadership' essay because every answer should depend on the question, not the topic. If you have a favourite topic that comes up in an essay question, make sure you read the question carefully and answer it rather than writing all you know about the topic.
- With few exceptions, A-level questions can be answered in two words: 'It depends.' Consequently, your main task in planning each essay is to consider what the answer depends on (e.g. the objectives of the organisation, internal or external constraints, the culture of the organisation).
- Essays need a structure that indicates where the answer is leading. A logical structure is to present your basic points, explaining and analysing them (using business theories and ideas), culminating in an overall weighing up of the evidence in order to create a reasoned conclusion that is supported by the evidence.
- The key to a good essay is that it is clearly and constantly focused on the question. Discipline yourself by referring back to the question regularly. This will be time well spent because it will help you to avoid including irrelevant detail and argument. Every paragraph in an essay should contribute to answering the question. Any paragraphs that are irrelevant or off the point are unlikely to earn you marks but will take up precious time.
- Analysis means using business concepts to answer questions with precision and depth. The ability to apply business theories and ideas, to break down a question in order to identify the key issues involved, and the use of relevant concepts will all lead to analysis marks being awarded.
- Evaluation is the key to really strong essays. With 40% of the marks for an essay being awarded for this skill, evaluation is twice as valuable as any other skill that you can demonstrate. Evaluation means showing judgement. For good marks you need to:

- demonstrate the ability to examine arguments critically and to highlight differing opinions
- distinguish between fact, well-supported argument and opinion
- weigh up the strength of different factors in an argument in order to show which you believe to be the most important and why
- show how the topic fits into the wider business, social, political or economic context

The following guidance will be useful when addressing the questions in both Section A and Section B:

- All questions in this unit require answers that demonstrate evaluation. This is reinforced by the instructions in the questions to 'discuss', 'evaluate', 'assess' or 'judge the extent to which'.
- In Section A, the questions ask you to make use of the context of the articles *and* your own research. This will involve applying the points you make to companies or contexts that you have explored and researched. If you fail to do this, you are unlikely to earn marks for application.
- Similarly, in Section B, the questions ask you to refer to a particular industry or type of business or any industry or business with which you are familiar as a context for your answer. This means you should try to use relevant business examples, theories, case studies or data to support your arguments. If you fail to do this, you are unlikely to earn marks for application.

Section A

The changing economic environment

Pre-issued research theme

In researching this area, you should consider issues such as:

- the key macroeconomic variables that affect businesses, including the business cycle, interest rates, exchange rates, inflation, unemployment and economic growth
- recent trends in each of these variables
- how changes to each of these variables might affect businesses
- how the impacts of these variables on businesses tends to be interlinked
- the strategies that business might deploy in response to changes in the economic environment
- recent and current examples of the impact of the economic environment on businesses

You are encouraged to study these issues in the context of business case studies.

Stimulus material

The following short article should be read prior to answering the question.

The recession in UK manufacturing deepened in February 2009. Figures from the Chartered Institute of Purchasing and Supply showed that levels of production and employment fell at record rates. Employment and output were at their weakest since 1992, with around 30,000 UK factory jobs being axed each month as firms cut costs in the face of weaker demand. Figures also showed an annual decline in manufacturing production of around 12%, with larger firms increasingly under pressure. Initially the recession hit small and medium-sized companies the worst, but larger manufacturers — especially those dependent on the automotive and construction sectors — were increasingly struggling. With bigger firms being so badly hit, jobs were being slashed at a record rate as firms tried to survive the unrelenting market conditions.

The dramatic fall in the value of sterling in the second half of 2008 added to the financial pressures faced by thousands of small businesses that deal overseas. About a fifth of the UK's export and import business is carried out by small and medium-sized firms, which represents overseas trade worth £141 billion. A weak pound is usually good news for exporters, but the recession and rising unemployment hit demand in the markets and the slump in sterling against the dollar and the euro affected profit margins. The rate of decline in new export orders accelerated sharply in February 2009. Despite the mitigating influence of a weaker pound, firms reported reduced demand from East Asia, the euro zone, the Middle East and the United States.

With reference to the article above *and* your own research, discuss the extent to which recession affects every type and size of business and evaluate the strategies businesses might take in response to a recession.

(40 marks)

The key words are 'discuss', 'recession' and 'evaluate'. It may be tempting to discuss the business cycle in general. Try to avoid this. Explaining the business cycle and its various phases briefly as an introduction is acceptable but the answer must then focus on 'recession'.

The question requires an answer in two parts. The first part should discuss the different ways in which recession affects different types of business. Conclude your discussion of this with a decision about whether recession actually does affect every type and size of business. The second part should identify and evaluate the various strategies different businesses might take to survive during a recession.

Student A

A business cycle is the regular pattern of rising and falling GDP in an economy over time. It includes four phases — a boom, a recession, a slump and a recovery. It looks like this:

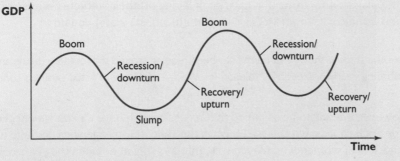

The business cycle

A boom is a period of high consumer demand, business confidence, profits and investment at the same time as rising costs, increasing prices and full capacity. A recession is a period of falling levels of consumer demand, output, profit and business confidence, little investment, spare capacity and rising levels of unemployment. The official definition of a recession is when there has been a fall in GDP for two consecutive quarters. A recession began in the UK in the second quarter of 2008 and is not showing any signs of improving (September 2011). A slump means very low levels of consumer demand, investment and business confidence, an increasing number of businesses failing and high unemployment. A recovery means slowly rising levels of consumer demand, rising investment, patchy but increasing business confidence and falling levels of unemployment.

This introduction indicates clearly that the student has a sound understanding of the business cycle and its phases and is able to explain them very well. The question is about recession so the examiner would expect the rest of the answer to focus only on recession and not on these other phases of the business cycle.

A recession can have really serious effects on businesses. Because incomes are falling, there is falling demand. If firms have excess stock or they are trying to keep their customers, they may reduce prices. During a recession, there are sales and price-related promotions all the time — closing down sales, 2 for 1 promotions etc. Falling demand and reductions in output may lead to low profits or even losses being made and workers being laid off. This then becomes a vicious circle because unemployment means incomes falling further and the circle starts again. Eventually businesses collapse as a result of falling demand and losses and even more workers are unemployed, incomes fall further, and so on.

ⓔ This paragraph demonstrates high-quality analysis. The student shows clearly that he/she understands the implications of recession on certain types of businesses, and is able to illustrate the linked processes of cause and effect — the essence of good analysis.

Examples of businesses affected by recession are numerous and every day in the newspapers there are examples of businesses that are going bust or laying off workers. The car industry has been hit by falling demand and this in turn is affecting their suppliers. Other firms that have been laying off their workers because of falling demand include BT, Virgin Media, GlaxoSmithKline, ITV and Vodafone.

ⓔ Here the student shows that he/she has been reading around the research theme and is demonstrating clearly his/her ability to apply knowledge of theory to actual business contexts.

However, it tends to be assumed that recession will have a negative effect on all types of business, but this isn't always the case. Nanny agencies do quite well because lots of women who may have wanted to stay at home in the years before their children start school feel they need to go back to work — this is especially the case if their husband has been made redundant. Shoe repairers do better because people think twice about throwing a pair of shoes away just because the heel has worn down and instead they go and get them fixed.

ⓔ This is another good paragraph that is clearly focused on the question and again demonstrates that the student is able to apply theory to real-world business contexts and uses these business contexts to support his/her arguments.

What all this means is that some firms are more vulnerable to changes in the business cycle than others because demand for their products or services is very closely linked to changes in income. For example, house builders are affected a lot because demand for houses is very closely linked with whether people's incomes are rising or falling. In a recession, when incomes are falling, there is very little demand for house building and many are likely to go out of business. The same is true of the services of people like carpenters and painters and decorators because people tend to put things on hold until they are confident they have the spare income to pay for this. Other businesses are less affected because the demand for their products isn't influenced very much by changes in income — for example, basic products like soap and milk. **a** This type of relationship between demand and income is known as income elasticity of demand and is similar to the concept of price elasticity of demand. In this case, if income changes and demand changes by a larger proportion, the product is income elastic, and if demand changes by a smaller proportion, the product is income inelastic. **b**

ⓔ **a** The excellent analysis of the previous paragraphs is allowing the student to make well-judged evaluative comments about how different firms are more or less vulnerable to changes in income and therefore to recession.

    b The student is using theory very well and, by illustrating this with real business examples, is demonstrating strong application skills.

    Other types of goods are affected in different ways. The demand for luxury goods, like foreign holidays or designer shoes, moves in the same direction as income — so when incomes are falling in a recession, demand for them falls because people need to spend their reduced incomes on more necessary goods. Some goods are known as inferior goods and the demand for these rises as incomes fall because people switch from buying luxury items to their low-priced substitutes. An example of this is Spam (pink tinned pork and ham meat). **c** The recession in America has led to an increase in the demand for this and, in fact, a recent newspaper article suggested that the makers of the meat have had to keep their factories working flat out to meet the demand. People are presumably buying this instead of more expensive meat such as fillet steak.

ⓔ **c** This is another excellent paragraph in which the student applies theory to a real business context, and thus illustrates how different types of businesses are affected by recession in different ways.

    Businesses need to have strategies to deal with a recession. **d** It is preferable that they think about this issue before a recession comes along as it is virtually impossible to change things for the better when demand and revenue are falling. **e** I have already explained that high unemployment will lead to a drop in demand for some goods and a switch in demand to other goods, such as inferior goods. This may lead firms facing falling demand to search for new markets. Indeed, one way to survive a recession for a producer of consumer goods is to diversify the product range. In this way the business is not too dependent for its profits on those products that are likely to experience wide variations in demand over the course of the business cycle. **f**

ⓔ **d** The student is now dealing with the second part of the question — about strategies a firm might take in response to a recession.

    e The initial point — that it is preferable for businesses to look ahead and be prepared rather than just responding — is excellent and shows that the student has a confident and sophisticated understanding of the issues.

    f Again there is very good analysis and evaluation in this paragraph.

During a recession, many businesses will suffer declining demand. As a result they will wish to reduce production and improve efficiency. For many this will mean laying off workers in order to reduce costs and survive. Although this may be an appropriate strategy in the short term, in the longer term losing experienced staff could become problematic, especially when demand begins to improve and experienced workers are difficult to find. Many firms in the current recession are asking workers to reduce their working time and take pay cuts in order to keep their jobs — this is good for workers because at least they keep their jobs, and is likely to retain their goodwill and benefit the business in the longer term. JCB did this by negotiating with the trade union that represents its workers to have a four-day week and a £50-a-week pay cut.

(e) Here is another excellent paragraph that focuses on the question, demonstrates high-quality analysis, well-chosen application of a business context to illustrate the point and thoughtful evaluation.

In conclusion, the question asks whether every type and size of business is affected by a recession. The answer is probably yes, but not in the same way. **g** Most businesses are adversely affected by a recession but some actually do quite well out of it. It really depends on the nature of the goods and services the business deals in, whether they are income elastic or inelastic and whether they are luxury or inferior goods. It also depends on the strategies they have in place to deal with the effects of a recession. If they can diversify into a range of products that have differing elasticities, this should help. If they have good relations with their workforce, they could introduce cost-saving strategies like JCB. **h** In the main though, in order to survive during a recession, businesses need to operate as efficiently as possible. They need a strong balance sheet, sufficient liquidity and low gearing. **i**

(e) **g** The conclusion refers back to the question and summarises the arguments made previously.
h Summarising the arguments made previously is a perfectly reasonable approach given that there has been plenty of evaluation throughout the essay.
i Unfortunately in the final sentence, a number of additional points are raised but not explained. It is impossible to know whether the student really understands why these points might benefit a firm in a recession. It may be that the student thought about these points at the last minute, by which time he/she had run out of time. Either way, they would not gain many additional marks.

(e) **Overall judgement: This answer is clearly A-grade standard. The student constantly focuses on the question and uses information from his/her own research. Convincing judgement based on sound analysis together with clear knowledge and understanding of theory and concept is evident throughout. The student's response to the second part of the question (about strategies) is much shorter than the first part, but the overall quality of argument means that this is not a problem.**

Student B

This question is about recession and how it affects business and what strategies businesses might take to deal with a recession. A recession is one of the phases of a business cycle. So first I will explain the business cycle and its causes, and then the implications of each phase of the cycle.

ℯ This introduction is not an encouraging start. The last sentence suggests that this answer may not be focused on the question.

A business cycle consists of the following phases:
- a boom, when income, demand and profits are high and inflation is rising
- a recession, when demand and profits are falling and unemployment is rising
- a slump, when demand is very low, businesses are failing and unemployment is high
- a recovery, when demand is rising and unemployment is falling

ℯ The student is demonstrating good knowledge and understanding of the business cycle. Given the question, it is perfectly reasonable to explain the business cycle in order to provide a context for the subsequent discussion of recession. However, a list of bullet points is never a good idea at A2, as it limits opportunities to demonstrate analysis and evaluation.

The business cycle is caused because of changes in business confidence, which lead to changes in the level of investment in fixed assets. If businesses don't replace their fixed assets because demand for their products is too low, firms that produce fixed assets, such as machinery, also suffer low demand. If low demand results in unemployment and low incomes, people reduce their spending on consumer durables (cars, washing machines and televisions), so firms that produce these also suffer.

ℯ This paragraph shows sound knowledge and understanding and good analysis about reasons for the business cycle — but the question does not ask for a discussion about the causes of the business cycle. Given the introductory paragraph, this is slightly worrying and suggests that the student is not going to address the question.

Implications of a boom:
- Because consumer demand is higher, it is likely to lead to increasing prices.
- Because demand is so high, there are likely to be shortages which will lead to cost increases e.g. wages may have to rise to keep skilled workers.
- Because of high demand, firms will be working at full capacity and may decide to expand.
- With increasing demand and prices, firms may earn increasing profit. **a**

Implications of a recession:
- Falling demand may lead to reduced prices.
- Falling demand and reduced output may lead to low profits or even losses and workers being laid off.

- Businesses might close because of falling demand and losses.
- Firms will have more bad debts and may need to introduce tighter credit control procedures, which may reduce demand for their products. **a**

Implications of a slump:
- The low level of demand means that businesses are likely to close, leading to large-scale unemployment. **a**

Implications of a recovery:
- Increasing demand may lead to increased profits and new business start-ups.
- Growing business confidence may mean more investment in fixed assets and more borrowing. **a**

(e) **a** These four sets of bullet points suggest that this student is simply writing all that he/she has learnt about the business cycle. No attempt has been made to tailor the discussion to the question. All that has been provided is a list of implications about each phase of the business cycle. The student should have provided a detailed analysis of the effect of recession on different types of businesses.

The strategies a business might use in response to changes in the business cycle will depend on which phase of the cycle the economy is in. **b** For example, during a recession, many businesses will suffer declining demand. As a result they will wish to reduce production and improve efficiency. For many this will mean laying off workers in order to reduce costs and survive. **c**

(e) **b** This suggests that the student has forgotten that the question is about recession and thinks that it is about the business cycle.

c The example relates to recession and demonstrates accurate analysis, but it is very brief and, as the second half of a 40-mark question, it is not sufficient.

Therefore the business cycle and the individual phases affect different businesses in different ways and, as a result, the strategies of different businesses in different phases will also differ.

(e) This sentence is true — but it is not what the question is about.

(e) **Overall judgement: This answer demonstrates good knowledge and understanding of the business cycle and its phases and includes some convincing analysis of this. However, it fails to include any application and hence shows no evidence of wider reading on the research theme. It does not address the question and includes no evaluation. There is no real depth of analysis at any stage, so this answer would be a clear U grade.**

Business ethics

Pre-issued research theme

In researching this area, you should consider issues such as:
- the meaning of business ethics
- the reasons businesses adopt ethical positions
- how businesses organise themselves when operating ethically and the strategies they might adopt
- the benefits, costs and risks for different businesses of adopting ethical positions
- the opportunities and threats facing businesses as a result of adopting ethical positions
- the impact on stakeholders of businesses adopting ethical positions
- the extent to which businesses adopting ethical positions do this as a public relations (PR) exercise or because of high moral principles
- recent and current examples of business ethic

You are encouraged to study these issues in the context of business case studies.

Stimulus material

The following short article should be read prior to answering the question.

A recent research report shows that companies that have a clear commitment to ethical conduct outperform those that do not. Using various indicators of business success, such as return on capital employed, it compared two groups of companies (those with a demonstrable commitment to ethical behaviour through having a published code of business ethics, and those without) over a four-year period. Overall, the companies with ethical codes were clearly superior. The report also suggests that having a code of ethics equates to a higher than average score in the ranking of Britain's Most Admired Companies and is therefore a strong proxy indicator of genuine ethical commitment and a well-managed company. Commentators suggested that the report supported the notion that not only is ethical behaviour in business life the right thing to do in principle, but that it pays off in financial returns.

The Co-operative Bank is an example of how ethical behaviour can benefit a company. More than 80,000 customers of the Co-operative Bank responded to a survey asking them for their views on the bank's ethical policy. Most wanted the bank to refuse loans to oppressive regimes and to companies that sell arms to oppressive regimes. Next on the list were companies that damage the environment by extracting and producing fossil fuels. As a result of the response, the bank has adopted stricter rules on lending to firms. The revised policy is expected to increase the number of loan applications turned down by the bank. Since introducing its ethical policy in 1992, rejected loans total over £1 billion. The policy, combined with its long-standing mutual status, is proving of benefit in the recession, with customers from rival banks transferring their accounts. Current accounts have increased by 65% since the beginning of 2008, and the increase in savings has allowed the bank to boost lending to customers by 15% to £4.4 billion.

With reference to the article above *and* your own research, assess the extent to which adopting an ethical position is simply good business practice and that so-called ethical organisations are simply using highly effective public relations strategies to attract customers. **(40 marks)**

ⓔ The key words are 'assess' and 'and' (before 'that so-called'). It will be tempting to discuss business ethics in general, but you should avoid this unless it forms just a brief introduction. Make sure that you answer the question and, in particular, that you address both issues mentioned — the extent to which adopting an ethical position is simply good business practice and the extent to which so-called ethical organisations are simply using highly effective public relations strategies to attract customers.

Student A

This essay will assess the extent to which adopting an ethical position is simply good business practice and whether so-called ethical organisations are simply using highly effective public relations strategies to attract customers.

ⓔ There is no need to restate the title.

Ethics are the moral principles that should underpin business decision making. A decision made on ethical grounds might mean that the most profitable solution for the business has been ignored in favour of one of greater benefit to society as a whole, or to particular groups of stakeholders.

Public relations (PR) involve activities to boost the public profile of an organisation and usually involve obtaining favourable publicity from the press, television or radio. Unlike advertising, it is not paid for and there is no control over its content. When a business behaves ethically, it may be good for PR. The title of the essay suggests that good PR might be the main reason for ethical behaviour because it can help to enhance the image of a business and is likely to generate more goodwill, which will lead to improved sales.

ⓔ These two introductory paragraphs demonstrate that the student clearly understands the key terms and they set the context for the rest of the essay.

Firms are frequently presented with ethical dilemmas when making decisions. For example, the extract talks about the Co-operative Bank, which has decided not to lend to organisations that support or sell arms to repressive regimes or organisations that damage the environment. Other firms that behave ethically include farming organisations that do not use factory farming methods, clothing manufacturers that refuse to make use of child labour and organisations that act responsibly towards the environment and are good employers.

ⓔ This paragraph indicates that the student is able to make use of examples other than simply those in the article provided and hence indicates that he/she has done some research on the theme.

Not all businesses adopt ethical approaches to their business, although few would say they do not. If a business sees its shareholders' or owners' short-term interests as its only responsibility or if it wants to charge the lowest prices in the market, it is likely to be meeting only its minimum obligations in relation to other stakeholder groups and the wider environment and thus is probably not behaving ethically. On the other hand, if a business takes an ideological approach to all its activities and places financial considerations secondary, it may not be very profitable but it is probably acting in a highly ethical manner.

e The student is demonstrating excellent understanding of ethical behaviour by discussing the spectrum of ethical approaches firms can take.

Regardless of moral principles, there are important commercial advantages to a business of acting ethically. For example, consumers often want the products of ethical companies more than those of others; ethical behaviour can thus become a USP for a business and can therefore be used in its marketing. For example, The Body Shop made its name this way and the Co-operative Bank is doing the same. Such a USP is likely to result in increased sales and, depending on costs, increased profits. Many highly qualified young people would prefer to work for an ethical company and therefore such companies are likely to be able to recruit the best and most motivated staff. In such a situation, whether a business is adopting an ethical approach or is simply using good business practice and effective PR is difficult to distinguish.

However, acting ethically can be expensive. For example, if a business chooses not to locate its production in a low-wage economy, this will mean its costs will be higher, so prices will rise and it might become less competitive and make less profits. From this point of view, one could argue that those businesses not clearly focused on ethical practices will opt for the cheapest and therefore the most profitable alternative.

e The discussion in the above two paragraphs of the advantages and problems facing firms adopting ethical behaviour demonstrates high-quality analysis. The points made are well developed, demonstrate very good use of knowledge from other areas of the specification and are well supported by business examples. The student also refers the points being made back to the original question, demonstrating that he/she is structuring the essay well in order to answer the question, rather than simply writing all he/she knows about business ethics.

Businesses operate in a highly competitive environment that influences their actions. A public outcry against a particular type of activity will force a business to look at itself and decide if it needs to change its stance. If a high-profile company, such as Nike or Gap, is accused of using child labour, other firms that produce in similar circumstances are likely to review their own operations and perhaps change to a more acceptable method of operation. Similarly, the recent accounting scandals will have caused many firms to take a closer look at their own accounting policies. One could argue that such reactions are just good business practice and a response to PR about unethical practice. Good business practice would suggest that a business benchmarks itself with the best in the industry. Benchmarking can also mean ensuring that your practice is not on a par with the worst.

ⓔ This paragraph demonstrates that the student has excellent knowledge of recent and current ethical issues in the business world. It also indicates that the student is able to utilise knowledge from other areas of the specification and to make sound judgements based on well-argued analysis.

> If a business behaves in what seems to be an ethical way, it is debatable whether this is a reflection of the business adopting a 'real' ethical position or a 'perceived' one, i.e. as a PR exercise in order to gain consumer loyalty and increase sales. But does it really matter, because the final outcome is that the business is behaving ethically? It isn't the case that the most profitable businesses are the least ethical or that the least profitable are the most ethical. In the latter case, it usually just means that they are not very good businesses and are not using good business practice. Perhaps good business practice means adopting an ethical approach and the fact that this may bring with it very beneficial PR is simply an added bonus.

ⓔ This is an excellent conclusion that demonstrates the student has brought all of the arguments included in the essay together in order to address the question.

ⓔ **Overall judgement: The student has written an excellent essay that is highly evaluative and includes well-argued analysis. This answer demonstrates excellent knowledge and understanding and an awareness of recent and current issues in relation to business ethics, although some of the application is rather general. Evidence of specific research is less obvious, so it would be a borderline A-grade response.**

Student B

> When a business adopts an ethical position it means that it is behaving morally and is not putting profit first. The Co-operative Bank in the article is an ethical business because it will not invest its money or make loans to businesses or governments that are not behaving morally — like oppressive regimes, companies that sell arms to oppressive regimes, and companies that damage the environment by extracting and producing fossil fuels.

ⓔ The student provides a rather simplistic explanation of the key term (ethical position), but the use of information from the article supports and reinforces this explanation.

> Businesses have to take the interests of their stakeholders into account. Stakeholders include shareholders, customers, suppliers, the local community and government. Each group of stakeholders will have different objectives and some of these will conflict.
> Shareholders will want the firm to achieve high profit levels either by keeping costs low or by charging high prices. High profits will in turn allow high dividends to be paid.
> Customers will want the firm to provide high-quality products and services at low prices, and to offer a good service and a wide choice.

Suppliers will want the firm to provide regular orders, prompt payment and steady growth, leading to more orders in the future.

The local community will want the firm to provide local employment opportunities and to behave in a socially responsible manner, safeguarding the environment and accepting the full social costs associated with its activities.

The government will want the firm to make efficient use of its resources, to provide employment and training, and to comply with legislation on consumer protection, competition policy, employment, and health and safety.

ⓔ The above six paragraphs demonstrate that the student has good knowledge and understanding about stakeholders. However, the paragraphs are very short and are essentially a list of points. More importantly, although taking into account the interests of particular groups of stakeholders could be a relevant issue in relation to ethical behaviour, this link has not been made yet.

Unethical businesses tend to focus on the needs of their shareholders and aim to make as much profit as possible. So they may decide to locate in another country and exploit cheap labour. This will help keep their costs down and keep their profits up.

Ethical businesses are more likely to focus on the needs of the local community and society in general — ensuring that they don't pollute the atmosphere or destroy the environment. As a result, their costs may be higher because they don't look for the cheapest way of doing things but look for the most ethically correct way. Because their costs are higher, their prices are often higher — like organic food — and they probably make less profit.

ⓔ The above two paragraphs illustrate some useful analysis about ethical and unethical behaviour. However, this analysis is not linked to the previous issue of stakeholders having conflicting needs. The student mentioned the issue of organic food, which might be relevant — but this is the only indication, so far, of any wider research on the issue of 'business ethics'.

Public relations are things like newspaper articles that inform the public about the business but that is not actually advertising because it is free and not paid for. An example of public relations would be the article about the Co-operative Bank if this appeared as a newspaper article. Some people might read it and think that it's a good bank to bank with, others might steer clear because from reading the article they will know they will be refused a loan because they are involved in unethical activities. So PR is a good way of letting people know what you're about without paying to do so. However, a business that is not ethical is unlikely to make this public because PR is not going to do anything for them.

ⓔ The student has a basic understanding of PR — as free publicity for a business — but is not really addressing the issue about ethical behaviour being good PR for a business.

> There are advantages for a business if it acts ethically. Sometimes consumers prefer to buy the goods and services of an ethical company because they think it reflects well on them and may make them look good or give them status. Making or selling ethical goods and services may lead to a good brand name which will help with marketing. Ethical companies are sometimes able to attract well-trained people. The problems for a business if it acts ethically are that it might be expensive because workers get higher wages and so costs and prices rise and profits fall.

ⓔ This paragraph demonstrates that the student understands how ethical behaviour can have an impact on a company. However, although relevant points are identified, they are not analysed and are not used effectively to address the question itself.

> In conclusion, adopting an ethical position is good business practice because it means that a firm is behaving properly and not exploiting anyone or any resources and not causing any damage to the environment.

ⓔ Although this conclusion refers back to the question, it does not demonstrate good analysis because the links it suggests are not necessarily the case — not exploiting workers or resources/ not damaging the environment might indicate ethical behaviour but the student has not explained why they indicate good business practice.

ⓔ **Overall judgement: The student clearly understands what ethical behaviour is and what an ethical business is, but he/she has not addressed the question. He/she has provided some relevant points and demonstrated reasonable analysis of some issues, however there is no indication that he/she has done any research or is aware of business examples (other than the mention of organic food and reference to the Co-operative Bank) and evaluation is weak. Consequently the limited application and evaluation marks mean a borderline U/E grade.**

Stakeholders

Pre-issued research theme

In researching this area, you should consider issues such as:
* the difference between shareholders and stakeholders
* different stakeholder perspectives
* the potential for conflict between different stakeholder groups
* the pressure stakeholders bring to decision making
* the relative power of stakeholders and their influence on corporate decision making

You are encouraged to study these issues in the context of business case studies.

Stimulus material

The following short article should be read prior to answering the question.

All the available evidence suggests that companies which are run with a view to the long-term interests of their key stakeholders are more likely to prosper than those which take a short-term, 'shareholder first' approach. The forces of economic globalisation and developments in the technology of mass communication will make stakeholder inclusion an increasingly essential component of corporate strategy in the twenty-first century. Put simply, companies, like governments and other established institutions, need to listen, to process and to respond positively to the values and beliefs of their stakeholders — most especially their customers, employees and investors. Failure to do this will reduce competitiveness and increase the risk of corporate decline.

An example of stakeholder involvement can be seen in Cadbury Schweppes, an international confectionery and beverages company, selling chocolate, sweets, gum and beverages around the world. Cadbury Schweppes' core purpose is 'working together to create brands people love' and some of its best-loved brands in the UK include Dairy Milk, Liquorice Allsorts, Jelly Babies, Flake, Roses, Trebor Mints and Wine Gums. In 2004, Cadbury Schweppes was voted 'Britain's Most Admired Company'. Cadbury Schweppes recognises that it does not operate in isolation and works at its commitment to each one of its stakeholders. It listens to its stakeholders and tries to balance their interests with the long-term benefits to the company. By engaging with stakeholders, it does more than sustain their goodwill and cooperation; it enables the company to remain competitive and successful, to keep in touch with wider social expectations, as well as making sure that the values of the company are upheld. Cadbury Schweppes knows that listening to and engaging with stakeholders in this way is essential to its success and, at the same time, has benefits for its stakeholders.

With reference to the article above *and* your own research, judge the extent to which meeting the needs of all stakeholders is crucial to business success.   (40 marks)

ⓔ The key words are 'judge the extent to which' and 'all'. Make sure that you answer the question, which is about whether meeting the needs of *all* stakeholders is important for business success. Avoid simply writing all you know about different stakeholders.

Student A

A stakeholder is an individual or group with a direct interest in the activities and performance of an organisation. The main stakeholders in a business are its owners and shareholders, others that provide finance, its employees (including managers), its customers, its suppliers and the local community.

Traditionally, firms only took into account the needs of their owners or, in limited companies, their shareholders. Over time, a number of organisations took a different view and aimed to meet the needs of other groups of stakeholders; for example, the John Lewis Partnership meets the needs of employees and the Co-operative Society aims to satisfy the needs of its customers. Nowadays, all firms are encouraged, by government and by pressure groups, to meet the wider needs of society by taking into account the externalities arising from their decisions.

ⓔ These two introductory paragraphs indicate that the student fully understands the term stakeholder and is also aware of how the significance of this concept has increased over time. The references to John Lewis and the Co-operative indicate that the student has researched this area and demonstrate his/her ability to apply concepts to real business situations.

To understand how varied and often conflicting the needs of different stakeholder groups are, I have listed the groups and given a brief analysis of their needs.
- Shareholders — want the firm to achieve high profit levels either by keeping costs low or by charging high prices. High profits will give them high dividends. They will also want the firm to have a positive corporate image and long-term growth because this will encourage share prices to rise.
- Employees — want job security, good working conditions, high levels of pay, promotional opportunities and job enrichment that gives them job satisfaction.
- Customers — want the firm to provide high-quality products and services at low prices, and to offer a good service and a wide choice.
- Suppliers — want the firm to provide them with regular orders, prompt payment and steady growth, leading to more orders in the future.
- The local community — wants local firms to provide plenty of local employment opportunities, to contribute to community activities and to behave in a socially responsible manner, avoiding or minimising any pollution or congestion from their activities.

ⓔ Although in general students are advised not to use bullet points or lists, in this instance, the approach enables the student to provide short but relevant information and analysis of the needs of each stakeholder group.

The above analysis indicates the level of conflict that a firm needs to deal with — consumers want low prices, employees want high levels of pay and shareholders want high profits. But low prices and high costs (wages) are likely to lead to low profits. It seems therefore that on a practical level, it is almost impossible for a business to meet all the needs of every stakeholder group. If a firm can't meet the needs of all stakeholder groups at the same time, it will have to set priorities and this is likely to lead to conflict which will affect the performance of the company and therefore its success. For example, if consumers don't get low prices, they will go to a competitor. If employees aren't paid high wages, they might leave and go to work for another company. If shareholders are not satisfied with the dividends they get from profits, they might sell their shares. It doesn't matter if a few do this, but if a lot do, share prices might fall and it could leave the company open to a takeover bid. If the company uses funds to provide social facilities or projects in the local community and these funds come out of profits, less is available for shareholders. If more rewards are directed towards the owners (shareholders), less are available for employees. If more rewards are given to managers in the form of bonuses, less might be available for workers. This last point has caused a lot of controversy in the banking sector, where even though banks have collapsed and workers have been made redundant, senior management still seem to be getting huge bonuses or pensions. The above analysis takes a 'win–lose' approach to the situation — it views the company as having a fixed amount of money that it has to share out among all stakeholder groups, so if one group gets more, another group has to get less. **a**

An alternative approach that avoids the problem of prioritising stakeholder needs is that of 'win–win'. Using this approach, a firm can, by being successful and using carefully thought-out strategies, ensure that the needs of all stakeholder groups are met. For example, in the case of Waitrose, better conditions and rewards for employees will increase their loyalty, their motivation, the quality of their work and enable Waitrose to charge higher prices. Starbucks' ethical behaviour towards coffee producers has also satisfied many of its customers, who in turn are prepared to pay higher prices. This has also served the needs of Starbucks' shareholders. Similarly, although paying suppliers on time might reduce cash flow, it is likely to ensure that the firm gets good service from its suppliers and can rely on them in an emergency. Recently Tesco has delayed payment to suppliers and this has lost it a lot of goodwill. **a b**

A firm that is socially responsible in the local community is likely to be able to put in plans for extensions to its sites and get these passed with less controversy because the local community is likely to respect them.

🄴 **a** The first and second paragraphs are rather long and could be broken down into shorter ones. However, their content is impressive. Although the student may have learnt about the win–lose and win–win approaches, these paragraphs cannot have been learnt by rote prior to the exam. They demonstrate how a thorough knowledge and understanding of the concepts and theory involved and a clear focus on the question allow the student to take a line of thought and develop it to reach a well-supported conclusion.

b The second paragraph also shows good evidence of research into actual businesses.

It seems that meeting the needs of all its stakeholders is crucial to a firm's success. Otherwise, those groups whose needs are not being met could take action that would adversely affect the firm. As mentioned, shareholders might sell their shares, which reduces share prices and possibly leads to a takeover. Experienced and skilled employees could leave and go to work with competitors, thus reducing productivity. Customers may take their custom elsewhere and the firm loses sales and revenue. Suppliers might go elsewhere or become unreliable in their delivery or the quality of their products. The local community may be antagonistic to the firm and therefore block any of its development plans that might affect the local area. However, it's a bit of a chicken and egg story, because the more successful a firm is, the more likely it is to be able to satisfy the needs of all of its stakeholder groups.

ⓔ This paragraph contains some repetition of points mentioned earlier but the judgements it makes as a consequence are both appropriate and well supported by evidence in this paragraph and in the answer as a whole.

The issue about stakeholders is present in all companies whether large or small, but it is particularly important in large organisations. Cadbury in the article tries to balance the interests of its stakeholders with the long-term benefits to the company. Similarly, a company like Tesco believes that if it operates efficiently and its customers are happy with what it provides, sales and profits will grow, which will be in the best interests of its shareholders. Some years ago, the founder of Greggs bakery said something about not putting the interests of shareholders before that of other stakeholders, which suggests that Greggs aims to ensure that it meets its customer needs first and expects that, by doing this, sales and profits will rise, which in the long term will benefit shareholders.

ⓔ This paragraph supports the previous conclusion and demonstrates that the student has researched the issue of stakeholders by exploring case studies of actual businesses.

It would seem therefore that in order to be successful, a business must be as effective at managing its stakeholders as it is at managing its market or financial position. As the article says, 'companies which are run with a view to the long-term interests of their key stakeholders are more likely to prosper than those which take a short-term, "shareholder first" approach'.

ⓔ This is a neat conclusion that makes use of the information provided in the article.

ⓔ **Overall judgement: This is a convincing A-grade answer. It demonstrates excellent knowledge and understanding, excellent research applied convincingly to actual business contexts, detailed and accurate analysis, and perceptive evaluation.**

Student B

A stakeholder is someone that has an interest in a business. They could be shareholders or workers or customers or other people like suppliers and investors and even pressure groups.

Historically, businesses really only aimed to please their shareholders — the owners of the business. This was done by ensuring that sufficient profit was made to ensure shareholders had good dividends. Of course this might lead to problems because by distributing too much of their profits to shareholders as dividends a business might leave insufficient retained profits to invest back into the business to develop and grow. The argument in favour of looking after shareholders was that if they weren't happy they could sell their shares. If this happened en masse, share prices would fall and it might mean that other firms might try to take over the business. So keeping shareholders happy was paramount.

e The student clearly understands the concept of stakeholders and is also aware of the historical emphasis on meeting the needs of shareholders.

But, of course, similar things can happen if other stakeholders are not happy. If workers are not getting a good deal in terms of their wages or their conditions of work they are likely to leave and try to find work with other firms. So the business will lose its skilled labour force and its productivity might drop. If customers don't like the products that are being made or find the prices too high or the quality too poor, they could just switch to another producer — assuming that the firm is not a monopolist and therefore the only supplier of the product. Both of these situations — workers and customers going to other firms — are likely to lead to a fall in profit, which is not going to benefit the shareholders or the company.

e This is valuable analysis and, together with the previous paragraph, suggests that the student is building an argument about the importance of meeting the needs of all stakeholders — the crux of the question.

The article talks about Cadbury and how it tries to look after its stakeholders by balancing their interests with the long-term benefits to the company. Other firms are probably exactly the same because none of them can afford to ignore their other stakeholders today. This is because stakeholders have a very strong influence on the decisions made by a business.

e Although there is nothing inaccurate in this paragraph, it is superficial. There is no mention of who the 'other firms' might be and hence no evidence of any research or application to real business contexts.

Pressure groups are stakeholders and they can exert a huge amount of influence on a business. A pressure group is a group of people with a common interest, who join together to achieve their goal by putting pressure on businesses. If a pressure group is seen by a business to represent the views of people affected by its activities, the actions of the pressure group and the pressure it puts on the business is likely to have more impact.

Pressure groups include single-issue pressure groups, such as a group against the construction of a particular road or building project such as an airport, and those with ongoing concerns, such as Greenpeace in relation to environmental issues and the consumers' association Which? in relation to the quality of products.

ⓔ These two paragraphs contain accurate information that is relevant to the question. Pressure groups are stakeholders and can and do influence business decision making. The assumption is that the student will use this aspect of stakeholder analysis in order to address the question.

Pressure group activity usually aims to change the actions of a business and thus to influence its decision making. The response a particular business might have to pressure group activity varies. Some companies agree to change. This might be because they are motivated by genuine ethically, socially or environmentally responsible beliefs, by a desire to protect the image of the company, or simply by a wish to avoid the costs that might be incurred in doing battle with a pressure group. Other companies might resist a pressure group's demands and launch a PR campaign to counter and discredit a pressure group's claims. Sometimes the government imposes change by passing new laws as a result of successful pressure group activities. For example, in the case of tobacco companies it might mean a ban on advertising on television and in other media, while in the case of a chemical company it might involve technical requirements to reduce emissions. Pressure group activity might persuade people to change their approach to the consumption or disposal of certain products, or the pollution that accompanies certain activities and thus they stop doing business with the company.

ⓔ The above paragraph makes it clear how a business could respond to pressure group activity, but it is not clear how this contributes to answering the question set. It seems that this student has learnt about pressure groups and is attempting to include his/her knowledge about them into an answer regardless of whether it is relevant to the question.

So overall, stakeholders have a lot of influence on a business. If a business cannot meet their demands, then, in order to remain successful, it must be strong enough to resist them while maintaining sales and the confidence of their customers and employees.

ⓔ The conclusion shows that the student has moved from a focus on the question — whether meeting the needs of all stakeholders is crucial to business success — to a focus on pressure groups and how a business should respond to them.

ⓔ **Overall judgement: This is an unsatisfactory answer and would not gain a pass grade. It is a classic example of a student trying to include aspects of business theory that have been learnt and have some relevance to the question, but that are not used appropriately or integrated effectively to answer the question.**

Leadership as a key influence on the management of change

Pre-issued research theme

In researching this area, you should consider issues such as:

- the meaning of leadership
- the distinction between leadership and management
- the range of leadership styles
- the internal and external factors influencing leadership styles
- the importance of leadership and its influence on the culture of an organisation
- the role of leadership in managing change
- the importance of leadership
- factors that promote and resist change

You are encouraged to study these issues in the context of business case studies.

Stimulus material

The following short article should be read prior to answering the question.

Jack Welch was Chairman and Chief Executive Officer of General Electric (GE) between 1981 and 2001. He gained a reputation for unique leadership strategies at GE and remains a highly regarded figure in business circles due to his innovative management strategies and leadership style. Jack Welch was about leadership, not management. He actually wanted to discard the term 'manager' altogether because it had come to mean someone who 'controls rather than facilitates, complicates rather than simplifies, acts more like a governor than an accelerator'. Welch gave a great deal of thought to how to manage employees effectively so that they were as productive as possible. He arrived at a seemingly paradoxical view. The less managing you do, the better off your company is. In other words, manage less to manage more. Welch decided that GE's leaders, who did too much controlling and monitoring, had to change their management styles. 'Managers slow things down. Leaders spark the business to run smoothly, quickly. Managers talk to one another, write memos to one another. Leaders talk with their employees, filling them with vision, getting them to perform at levels the employees themselves didn't think possible. Then they simply get out of the way.'

In May 2009, in discussing the recession and the role of leadership in the *Director* magazine, Jack Welch commented that most leaders did not see the recession coming, did not anticipate its scale, and do not know when it will end. He noted that in normal times, the central challenge of leadership is that of balancing the company's short- and long-term needs. He observed that today, however, most managers are fixated on the short term — reducing staffing, slashing costs and squeezing productivity by asking remaining employees (who are feeling frantic about job security) to double their effort — in order to survive. As a consequence, many leaders are neglecting to define and create the future for their companies. He forecast that when the upturn arrives, the business landscape will be different, there will be fewer competitors and perhaps more opportunity, but only for those companies that are primed and ready to seize it.

With reference to the article above *and* your own research, discuss the difference between leadership and management in the successful management of change and assess whether any one leadership style is likely to be more effective in meeting the challenges companies face in trying to manage change successfully.

(40 marks)

e The key words are 'discuss', 'leadership and management', 'management of change' and 'assess'. Ensure that you relate your discussion about leadership and management to the management of change, as the question requests.

The question requires an answer in two parts. The first part should discuss the difference between leadership and management in the successful management of change. The second part should assess whether any particular leadership style is likely to be more effective in managing change successfully.

Student A

First I will discuss the difference between leadership and management and the successful management of change, then leadership styles in relation to the successful management of change. I will then bring these together by discussing the management of change and how important leadership is in ensuring the process is successful.

e If time is pressing, there is no real need for an introduction like this. However, it does suggest that the student is marshalling his/her thoughts about the issues and structuring the response in order to address each aspect of the question.

Leadership means deciding on the objectives for a company and inspiring staff to achieve those objectives. Management means getting things done by organising other people to do it. Another way of looking at the difference between leadership and management is that leaders seize opportunities and managers avert threats. Jack Welch in the article suggests that one of the important responsibilities of leadership is to balance the short-term and long-term needs of a company and to be constantly looking ahead and defining and creating the future.

e The student is demonstrating good levels of knowledge and understanding about leadership and management and is making reference to the article.

The best leaders are often charismatic and seem to gain huge respect from their employees and from the public generally — they include business leaders such as Jack Welch, Philip Green, Alan Sugar or Richard Branson, or football managers such as Arsene Wenger or Alex Ferguson. They are often risk takers and people who can inspire people, but it is usually their management team that ensures their ideas are put into practice.

ⓔ The student is demonstrating his/her research on this subject by the ability to apply his/her knowledge to a range of business and football leaders.

In reality both leadership and management are required in order to manage change successfully. Leadership is about getting people to abandon their old habits and achieve new things, and therefore is largely about change — about inspiring, helping and sometimes enforcing change on people. But managers need to be able to organise and implement change and ensure, for example, that there is excellent communication in place, that the workforce does not feel threatened and that current activities continue to run smoothly.

In terms of managing change, both leaders and managers have an important part to play to ensure that it is successful. Leaders need the vision to identify the necessary change and the persuasive skills to carry it off. Managers need to be able to plan the change and ensure systems are in place to make it happen and to constantly review and evaluate it.

ⓔ The student is now demonstrating very good levels of knowledge and understanding about leadership and management, is applying this effectively to the particular focus of the questions, i.e. about the management of change, and is analysing and evaluating the issues well.

Leadership styles are the manner and approach of the head of an organisation or department towards his or her staff. The main leadership styles are:
- Authoritarian leadership — an approach which assumes that information and decision making should be kept at the top of the organisation. Authoritarian leaders employ formal systems with strict controls, giving out orders, rather than consulting or delegating. This is equivalent to McGregor's Theory X style.
- Paternalistic leadership — an approach where leaders decide what is best for their employees. The workforce is treated as a family — there is close supervision, but real attempts are made to gain the respect and acceptance of employees. This is really a type of authoritarian leadership style, but with leaders trying to look after what they perceive to be the needs of their subordinates.
- Democratic leadership — is related to Maslow's higher-level needs and Herzberg's motivators. It means running a business or a department on the basis of decisions agreed by the majority and means that leaders delegate a great deal, discuss issues, act upon advice and explain the reasons for decisions. This is equivalent to McGregor's Theory Y style.
- Laissez-faire leadership — an approach where the leader has minimal input in the decision-making process and essentially leaves the running of the business to the staff. This style often arises as a result of poor or weak leadership and a failure to provide the framework necessary for a successful democratic approach.

ⓔ Here the student demonstrates excellent knowledge and understanding about leadership styles, and is able to make appropriate reference to aspects of theory learnt in other parts of the AS and A2 course. However, it is not specifically related to the question.

An appropriate leadership style is vitally important if an organisation is to be successful in managing change. However, it is almost impossible to judge which would be the best style as it depends entirely on the particular context. For example:

- Where the successful management of change requires very quick action because the company is under significant pressure, leaders will have to take rapid and difficult decisions. Authoritarian leadership is likely to be effective in this situation. Ryanair chief executive Michael O'Leary is known as a decisive leader who is prepared to make quick decisions.
- A paternalistic leadership style might be effective when the management of change involves difficult decisions that affect employees because, in general in a company where this sort of approach is used, workers usually recognise that leaders are trying to support their needs as much as they can and thus they are likely to remain loyal. Arsene Wenger, of Arsenal, has built the club on the basis of loyalty to players who have tended to return that loyalty.
- A major advantage of democratic leadership is that the participation of workers in decision making allows input from people with relevant skills and knowledge, which is likely to ensure that change is planned and implemented properly as well as keeping people motivated. However, this decision-making style can be slower, which slows down the rate at which change is introduced.
- A laissez-faire approach is probably the least effective style when change needs to be introduced because in order to introduce and manage change successfully, a structure and systems and strong leadership are needed — which isn't the case under a laissez-faire regime.

ⓔ This paragraph demonstrates very good application of knowledge about leadership styles to the specific question posed. Although bullet points are being used, they are not a superficial list of items but, instead, each bullet includes substantial analysis in support of the statement that it is almost impossible to judge which style is the most effective.

Change management is the anticipation, organisation, introduction and evaluation of modifications to business strategy and operations. Appropriate leadership is an essential element of the successful management of change. But in addition, the following issues will affect the amount of resistance to change and therefore the ability of leaders to introduce and manage change successfully — clear objectives and mission so that the company knows where it is going, an appropriate and sufficient level of resources for change to be implemented and managed successfully, appropriate trained staff with relevant expertise and an appropriate organisational culture. **a** Philip Green has made radical changes at Topshop in order to improve its reputation as a 'fast fashion' shop. This philosophy has been adapted from the leadership approach of Amancio Ortega, who led the growth of fashion chain Zara.

ⓔ a The issues raised in this paragraph are not always developed sufficiently, particularly the issue about organisational culture.

Change is a constant feature of business activity. The key issues are whether potential change has been foreseen by the company — and therefore planned for — and whether it is within the company's control. The current recession and the impact of falling incomes and demand were not foreseen by most firms and they have found it very hard to cope with. However, some leaders, such as Terry Leahy at Tesco, do appear to have anticipated the recession. He has led a broadening of Tesco's product range, so that Tesco has remained competitive by entering a price war with Asda. The issue that Jack Welch raises about looking to the future even in a period of recession when present strategies are focused on survival is an important issue and suggests that actually leadership needs to be able to take on board aspects of the different styles in order to meet the present and future needs of the business. For example, it needs to be decisive in ensuring that the business survives in the current economic climate; it needs to be paternalistic in ensuring that workers recognise that their needs are fully considered, meaning they are likely to remain loyal; it needs to be democratic so that a diverse range of views are taken into account leading to better decision making, improved motivation and trust, and a workforce that is more willing to accept, and even welcome, change. In addition, leaders need to have highly effective leadership skills and not just management skills. Management skills are more likely to ensure that the day-to-day operations are working effectively so that the company can survive in the current climate. In the situation of recession, leaders need to take the long view and need to be looking to the future to ensure that the company can take advantage of opportunities when they eventually emerge.

It is not always possible to define the reasons behind a leader's success. Howard Schultz led Starbucks for 15 years before handing over leadership to a colleague. However, after 2 years of poor trading, Schultz is back in charge and introducing new strategies aimed at re-establishing Starbucks' dominant position. Starbucks' successes are closely related to his periods of leadership.

ⓔ This is a highly analytical and evaluative conclusion that relates directly to the question. Using the context of recession and planning for the future are interesting issues and demonstrate a thoughtful approach. The student has managed to pull together both aspects of the question skilfully and perceptively. The final judgements — that effective leadership needs to take on board aspects of all leadership styles and that leadership rather than management is the key to success in the long term — are very persuasive.

ⓔ **Overall judgement: This is an interesting essay and a definite A grade. The student demonstrates excellent knowledge and understanding, and is able to apply this effectively to each aspect of the question posed, with numerous real-life examples. Strong analysis of issues is provided throughout most of the answer and evaluation of issues is particularly strong at the end of the answer.**

Student B

Leadership is doing the right thing and management is doing things right. Leadership is about getting people to abandon their old habits and achieve new things, and therefore largely about change — about inspiring, helping and sometimes enforcing change in people.

ⓔ This initial paragraph suggests the student has good knowledge and understanding of the various concepts involved.

> Some experts suggest that managers have subordinates but leaders have followers. In this context, managers have a position of authority vested in them by the company, and their subordinates work for them and largely do as they are told. Managers and workers therefore have what is known as a transactional relationship i.e. the manager tells the subordinate what to do, and the subordinate does this because they have been promised a reward. On the other hand, leaders do not have subordinates, other than those who are also managers. Although leaders have followers, telling people what to do will not inspire them to follow. In order to get people to follow them, a leader needs to appeal to them and show them how following them will lead to transformational benefits; for example, that followers will receive not just extrinsic rewards (such as wages and salaries) but intrinsic benefits such as somehow becoming better people. Thus, leaders realise the importance of enthusing others to work towards their vision.

ⓔ This paragraph continues to suggest that the student has good knowledge and understanding of the concepts of leadership and management. In a generic sense, it also analyses the implication of these concepts for an organisation well. However, there is no attempt to apply these concepts either to real-world scenarios or to the idea of the management of change, which is an essential element of the question.

> There are four main categories of leadership style that are used widely. These include authoritarian, paternalistic, democratic and laissez-faire styles of leadership.
> Authoritarian leadership assumes that information and decision making should be kept at the top of the organisation. Authoritarian leaders employ formal systems with strict controls, giving out orders rather than consulting or delegating. This may happen because leaders have little confidence in the ability of their staff or because they are simply unable to, or prefer not to, relinquish power and control. It may, however, reflect significant pressures on the organisation that force leaders to make rapid and difficult decisions. This is often the case in crisis or emergency situations, where an authoritarian approach is often the most effective. The advantages of this approach are that there are clear lines of authority and it can result in quick decisions. However, it can cause frustration and resentment because the system is so dependent on the leader and because of the non-participation of workers in the decision-making process.
> Paternalistic leadership is essentially an approach where leaders decide what is best for their employees. The workforce is treated as a family — there is close supervision, but real attempts are made to gain the respect and acceptance of employees. This is really a type of authoritarian leadership style, but with leaders trying to look after what they perceive to be the needs of their subordinates. Leaders are likely to explain the reasons for their decisions and may consult staff before making them, but delegation is less likely to be encouraged. The main advantage is that workers recognise that leaders are trying to support their needs.

Democratic leadership means running a business or a department on the basis of decisions agreed by the majority. In some situations this can mean actually voting on issues, but it is more likely to mean that leaders delegate a great deal, discuss issues, act upon advice and explain the reasons for decisions. Democratic leaders not only delegate, but also consult others about their views and take these into account before making a decision. The major advantage of democratic leadership is that the participation of workers in decision making allows input from people with relevant skills and knowledge, which may lead to improved morale and better-quality decisions. However, the decision-making process might be slower because of the need to consult and discuss, and there might be concern as to where power lies and whether loss of management control is a danger.

Laissez-faire leadership is an approach where the leader has minimal input in the decision-making process and essentially leaves the running of the business to the staff. Delegation occurs in the sense that decisions are left to people lower down the hierarchy, but such delegation lacks focus and coordination. This style often arises as a result of poor or weak leadership and a failure to provide the framework necessary for a successful democratic approach. However, there may be a conscious decision to give staff the maximum scope to use their initiative and demonstrate their capabilities. How effective it is depends on the staff themselves — some will love the freedom to use their initiative and to be creative whereas others will hate the unstructured nature of their jobs. This can be an effective style when employees are highly skilled, experienced and educated, when they have pride in their work and the drive to do it successfully on their own, and when they are trustworthy and experienced. The style is less effective when it makes employees feel insecure, when leaders fail to provide regular feedback to employees on how well they are doing, and when leaders themselves do not understand their responsibilities and are hoping that employees can cover for them.

ⓔ The above four paragraphs demonstrate excellent knowledge and understanding of leadership style and also high-quality analysis of how this impacts on business. However, there is no attempt to link this to the management of change.

Another way of analysing leadership style is to use McGregor's Theory X and Theory Y model.

McGregor's Theory X manager is an authoritarian leader who assumes that workers: are lazy, dislike work and are motivated by money; need to be supervised and controlled or they will underperform; have no wish or ability to help make decisions or take on responsibility; are not interested in the needs of the organisation and lack ambition.

McGregor's Theory Y manager is a democratic leader who assumes that: workers have many different needs, enjoy work and seek satisfaction from it; workers will organise themselves and take responsibility if they are trusted to do so; poor performance is likely to be due to boring or monotonous work or poor management; workers wish to, and should, contribute to decisions.

ⓔ These paragraphs continue to demonstrate the student's excellent knowledge and understanding, but neither application nor analysis is being shown here.

An appropriate leadership style is vitally important if an organisation is to be successful. Probably the worst situation is where an authoritarian approach is used with highly skilled and experienced staff in normal circumstances, as this is likely to alienate staff. Equally, a very democratic or even laissez-faire style of leadership in an emergency situation, or where workers are inexperienced and unskilled, is likely to lead to real problems.

(e) As a conclusion, this is a well-judged paragraph in relation to leadership style in general, but it does not refer to the management of change and hence does not answer the question posed.

(e) **Overall judgement: This is a disappointing answer and is likely to earn a U grade. The student clearly has excellent knowledge and understanding of the difference between leadership and management and of the various leadership styles. However, there has been no attempt to apply this knowledge to the question posed and no attempt to demonstrate awareness of real-world context. An answer that shows no evidence of independent research, such as this one, can be awarded only Level 1 application and evaluation. This means the maximum total available is limited to 22 marks. Although there is some good analysis of issues, these are not contextualised to the issue raised in the question — the successful management of change. It is as if the student has learnt by rote a prepared answer on leadership but has ignored the question.**

Section B

Question 1

> With reference to the car industry, or any other industry with which you are familiar, discuss the elements that make up 'the external environment' that it faces and how an individual firm in the industry might take these elements into account in its corporate planning process. (40 marks)

ⓔ The key words are 'car industry, or any other industry with which you are familiar', 'discuss' and 'and'. The question requires an answer in two parts. The first part should discuss the elements that make up the external environment that the car industry or another industry faces. The second part should discuss how an individual firm in the chosen industry might take the elements identified into account in its corporate planning process.

Student A

All businesses operate in a constantly changing external environment that consists of a wide and varied range of elements. This can be shown by the following diagram:

The business and its environment

This shows that business operates first within a competitive environment. The nature of this competition varies from industry to industry. The number of competitors, for example, dictates the extent to which a business can raise or lower its prices and the amount of advertising it is likely to undertake.

The business also operates within a general business environment, which involves the broader influences that affect all businesses, including issues such as the impact of changes in government policy on business, how legislation influences business behaviour, and the extent to which technological change and environmental considerations affect the type of products that are demanded and the way in which they are produced.

ⓔ This introduction demonstrates clear understanding of the 'external environment' but as yet there is no mention of the car industry or any other industry.

The competitive environment of the car industry is an oligopoly. This means there are a small number of large producers in the industry. The 5-firm concentration ratio is very high, with the largest five firms having over 80% of the market. The top three are Nissan, Toyota and Honda. Using Porter's five forces model to analyse the industry suggests the following:

Power of suppliers tends to be weak because they are large in number and often small in size, which is one of the reasons why when car manufacturers collapse there is such a huge knock-on effect on their component suppliers.

Power of buyers tends to be weak because they are large in number and small in size — mainly being individual buyers.

Substitutes include alternative forms of transport but, for any one manufacturer, they also include alternative makes of cars, so there is always intense competition.

Barriers to entry into the industry are high — car plants need to operate on a huge scale in order to reap economies of scale, capital set-up costs, establishing a network of dealerships and marketing to establish a name that people trust. All of this is hugely expensive and prevents new firms from entering the industry and setting up in competition.

(e) The above paragraphs suggest impressive knowledge of the car industry, and the use of relevant theory — Porter's five forces — helps in structuring an appropriate analysis of the competitive structure of the industry.

In order to structure my discussion of the broader external environment facing the car industry, I am going to use a PESTLE analysis. This is a framework for assessing the likely impact of the political, economic, social, technological, legal and environmental factors in the external environment of a business. For the car industry these categories are likely to include the following issues:

- Political factors — taxation and duties; subsidies and other financial support
- Economic factors — excess capacity; economies of scale; mergers and joint ventures; east Asian competitors/globalisation; level of concentration; the business cycle; the range of substitutes available
- Social factors — green options in relation to fuel choice; fashions and taste; lifestyle choices
- Technological factors — e-commerce and purchasing; safety issues; plant efficiency; fuel technology
- Legal factors — legislation relating to: environmental issues; company cars; competition policy
- Environmental factors — carbon dioxide emissions; congestion and pollution; road widening

(e) The student demonstrates an impressive knowledge of the external environment facing the car industry. However, the use of a relevant model (PESTLE) to structure the analysis in this way means that many individual points are merely listed. Consequently only content can be rewarded, as there is no analysis of the PESTLE factors at this point.

The above list indicates that a range of external factors are affecting the car industry. However, at the moment, the most significant is the impact of the recession, which is affecting the very survival of most manufacturers.

Recession means that incomes, and therefore demand, are falling. Cars are a luxury item but also when people have less money to spend they tend to hold on to their existing cars for longer. This situation means that the car industry is faced with falling demand. The news has been full of reports of car manufacturers making their workforce redundant or getting them to work less hours and/or take pay cuts. It seems as if it has affected all parts of the market from large expensive cars to smaller ones. As a result of this, in 2009–10, the government stepped in (in America as well as in the UK) to support the industry. People were being offered £2,000 if they got rid of their old car and bought a new one. This was to encourage the demand for new cars.

ⓔ Having identified a large range of external factors in the previous section, the student has identified what he/she considers to be the most significant one and has provided detailed analysis and evaluation of this issue.

The issues mentioned above can be classified as the political and economic issues. Another major influence has been environmental issues. For many years, the government has made it so that car and petrol taxation favours those people driving more environmentally friendly vehicles. Most people are well aware of the need to consider environmental issues when buying and using cars, and hence they have wanted to buy cars that produce fewer emissions. For the same reason many people make more use of public transport rather than using cars. Congestion charging, for example in London, stops so many people bringing their cars into towns. Manufacturers are aware of the environmental issues and, through technological developments, they are ensuring that the production methods used to make new cars are more environmentally friendly and the cars themselves produce less carbon dioxide emissions.

ⓔ Further high-quality application, analysis and evaluation are provided here. The student's strategy to select two issues from his/her PESTLE list and consider them in more detail is a good one. Although candidates would be expected to demonstrate that they understand the extent of the external environment and broadly what elements it involves, they would not be expected to consider every element in detail. The fact that the student selected the two that are currently most significant is well judged.

The question asks how an individual firm might take the external environment into account in its corporate planning process. The corporate planning process involves a firm in producing a plan of action that will allow it to meet its corporate objectives. The plan usually makes use of the information in a SWOT analysis. A SWOT analysis is a structured approach to assessing the internal and external influences on corporate plans. It identifies the key internal strengths and weaknesses of the firm and its external opportunities and threats, and analyses what the firm needs to do to counter threats, to seize opportunities, to build on its strengths and to overcome its weaknesses.

My previous analysis indicates the elements in the external environment of the car industry. By identifying these elements and analysing their possible implications, a business should be able to see what opportunities and threats it is likely to face. This should mean that its corporate planning is better because it is better informed. For example, knowing that demand is falling and therefore competition is likely to be intense, firms will need to consider price-cutting strategies. Cutting prices means they will need to be as efficient as possible, and hence may need to cut any excess capacity including cutting the workforce. However, their planning must not just take account of the present and what is best to do now in order to survive. It also needs to take account of the future and what will happen when economic recovery occurs — will they be in a position to seize opportunities and increase production to meet demand? Hence, a number of firms have cut the working week rather than make their workers redundant.

ⓔ In these last two paragraphs, the student ensures that he/she sticks tightly to the question so that all elements are fully addressed. He/she demonstrates well how the previous analysis of the external environment might contribute to corporate planning.

ⓔ **Overall judgement: This is a convincing A-grade answer. It shows secure knowledge and understanding of concepts and relevant theory, and the quality of analysis is excellent. The student's ability to apply his/her knowledge and understanding of theory and of the industry to the particular focus of the question is impressive and leads to well-judged evaluation.**

Student B

A PESTLE analysis is a way of analysing the external environment of any firm. It consists of the political, economic, social, technological, legal and environmental element.

ⓔ This introduction suggests that the student understands what issues should be considered in order to respond to the question.

A PESTLE analysis would look like this:

Political factors
- government economic policies
- government social policies
- the extent of government intervention

Economic factors
- the business cycle
- interest rates
- exchange rates
- the level of inflation
- the level of unemployment
- membership of the EU

Social factors
- ethical issues
- the impact of pressure groups
- the influence of different stakeholders
- changing lifestyles

Technological factors
- new products
- new processes
- the impact of change
- the costs of change

Legal factors
- legislation

Environmental factors
- environmental issues

These factors affect all organisations and industries, including the car industry.

ⓔ Using the PESTLE analysis, the student has accurately identified the type of issues that might be considered in the external environment of any industry. However, there is no attempt to analyse any of these issues or to apply them to the car industry or an industry chosen by the student. Thus only marks for knowledge and understanding have been earned so far. Even for a 40-mark question, it is advisable to focus on perhaps four or five issues in detail, rather than give a list that consumes valuable time.

A corporate plan is a plan to meet the aims and objectives of a business. The advantages of a corporate plan are that it allows for better coordination of activities within a business. It also helps to identify the resources required by a business and so makes it easier to raise finance by providing a clear plan of action, indicating how and why investment is required. Its success depends on a number of issues, including whether it is the right plan for the business in its present circumstances, whether there are adequate financial, human or production resources to implement the plan, the probable actions and reactions of competitors, and how changes in the external environment are likely to affect the plan and the business.

ⓔ There is no doubting the student's knowledge and understanding of the concepts and theory mentioned in the question, i.e. the external environment and corporate planning. However, there is no application and no sense in which the student is trying to answer the question.

The corporate planning process involves the following stages:
- mission statement
- objectives
- internal environment
- external environment
- SWOT analysis
- strategic choice
- strategic implementation
- control and evaluation

ⓔ Including this level of factual detail without applying it to the question suggests that the student has learnt a lot of information on corporate planning and is determined to include it, regardless.

> So analysing the external environment is an important stage in the corporate planning process because it contributes to the SWOT analysis. A SWOT analysis is a technique that allows a business to assess its overall position by reviewing an audit of its internal position and its external position. The internal audit involves an assessment of the strengths and weaknesses of a firm in relation to its competitors. It looks at current resources, how well they are managed and how well they match up to the demands of the market and to competition. The external audit involves an assessment of the opportunities and threats facing a firm in the general business environment. One method of analysing these external factors is to categorise them according to a PESTLE analysis, which I have done above.
>
> Therefore an analysis of the external environment contributes to a firm's SWOT analysis, which in turn contributes to a firm's corporate planning process.

ⓔ The student indicates clearly how, in a general sense, the external environment contributes to corporate planning. However, there is still no attempt to apply it to the car industry or any other industry, and thus there is very little analysis and no evaluation. The conclusion simply restates what has already been said.

ⓔ **Overall judgement: The student's knowledge and understanding of the main business concepts mentioned in the question is good and he/she clearly understands how they are linked together. However, this is a weak answer because there is no attempt to apply knowledge and understanding of concepts to the context of either the car industry or an industry of the student's choice and, as a result, analysis is superficial and there is no evaluation. The answer would not earn a pass grade.**

Question 2

Discuss the factors that an electrical retailer, or any other business with which you are familiar, would consider in deciding whether to pursue growth by taking over or merging with another business.   (40 marks)

ⓔ The key words are 'Discuss', 'electrical retailer, or any other business with which you are familiar' and 'pursue growth'. This question is about whether a business that wishes to grow should do so via a takeover or a merger. If you conclude that neither would be suitable and that organic growth would be more effective, ensure that your conclusion is soundly argued.

Student A

Takeovers and mergers can be horizontal, vertical or a form of diversification. A horizontal takeover would involve the buying of a competitor, such as Currys buying Comet. Vertical would mean integration with a supplier or a customer. As the firm in question is a retailer, this would have to be an example of backward vertical integration (taking over a supplier). Diversification means buying a firm in a different line of business.

ⓔ This is a good introduction, defining or clarifying many of the terms needed in the essay.

The reasons for the takeover will depend on which of the above applies. Horizontal integration will help a firm to gain control of the market. If the firm can eliminate its competition, then it can charge whatever price it likes and so maximise profit. However, in the UK the Competition Commission has the power to prevent a takeover if it thinks that this will happen. If the new company owned more than 25% of the market it is probable that it would be blocked. Thus the predicted reaction of the Competition Commission is a major factor that would be considered by an electrical retailer.

ⓔ This is a strong paragraph, demonstrating both application and analysis, drawing on the student's knowledge of both the business world and business theory and concepts. This has allowed an early evaluation of one of the key factors.

Horizontal integration leads to economies of scale — larger companies can buy in bulk, get cheaper loans and so on, helping them to undercut the competition. If price is important to the customers, this could be the major reason for the takeover. However, the retailer must be careful. Many mergers fail because the firm becomes too large, suffering from diseconomies of scale such as poor communication. In general, electrical retailers seem to compete fiercely on price and so a takeover would be a good idea, but not if the firm has a reputation for customer care and individual service — this could be damaged by a takeover.

(e) This paragraph offers further reasoning and good analysis, but the argument has tailed off quickly without really saying why a takeover might damage reputation. Still, there is evidence of evaluation in the cautious use of language.

Vertical integration could be very useful too. This would guarantee the retailer first choice of supplies. Taking over a manufacturer would improve its ability to offer after-sales service and to provide specialist products, tailor-made to the customer specification. This would increase the profit margin. The retailer could use special offers on its own brands to entice more people into the shop.

(e) This paragraph contains more analysis, but there is scope for evaluation of these factors. Unfortunately the student has not seized the opportunity this time.

Diversification would help to spread risks. In a recession sales may drop and so a takeover of a supermarket, for example, would help it to overcome difficulties.

(e) There is a lot left unsaid here. Do not expect the examiner to make up your line of argument for you. Show why a recession would be more of a problem for an electrical retailer than a supermarket and then tie this into the reasons for the takeover.

There are many other factors to consider in a takeover. The culture of the two firms would need to be merged. A power culture in one firm might not go well with a task culture in the other, and a disunited company could create problems for the new firm.

(e) These brief paragraphs have potential but would not be rewarded as much as a more focused and fully developed line of argument would be.

Sometimes a takeover allows a firm to acquire valuable assets, such as patents or brand names. This is not likely to apply so much to retailers, but if one has obtained good locations then this could be a factor. **a** The government is now making it more difficult for businesses to locate in out-of-town centres and so a firm might be very keen to buy another business that has a lot of sites that it could not get in any other way. **b**

(e) **a** The opening sentence introduces an issue but then rejects it as not relevant. This is an acceptable way of evaluating as long as some valid points are made and supported.
b The final sentence demonstrates very good awareness of the particular business context — electrical retailer — and leads to a sound judgement.

The price of the shares would be an issue. If share prices are low it might be possible to buy a firm cheaply (but harder to raise the money to do it).

(e) This is relevant but far too brief. This could have been an evaluative argument if set against other factors. For example, showing how the opportunity to acquire out-of-town sites might not have been worth it if the share price was prohibitively high, thus losing the company too much money. Essays can sometimes test the skill with which a student uses ideas as much as the ability to come up with relevant ideas.

> In conclusion, the factors to be considered will depend on the circumstances. If a profit can be made, it is more likely to go ahead. **c** Surveys indicate that the most successful takeovers are those involving firms of a similar size, and so this should be considered. It is much easier to understand the needs of a similar firm, and the two sets of employees are more likely to see it as a merger, rather than one company forcing its policies on another.

ⓔ **c** The second sentence on profit is a bit weak without any other commentary, but is still worth saying because it will nearly always be true.

> There must be no detrimental effects. The firm will need a healthy cash flow, and there must be scope for efficiencies. In this case it may wish to rationalise the number of outlets, to cut costs without losing sales revenue. Alternatively, the takeover might work well if the two firms are not in direct competition (e.g. in different areas), but can benefit from economies of scale.
> The final decision will depend on the owners of the two firms. The shareholders of the firm being taken over must be offered an attractive price for their shares, while the larger firm's shareholders must be convinced that it will benefit them too.

ⓔ The final paragraphs show good reasoning, but the arguments lack some application.

ⓔ **Overall judgement: This student shows a stronger grasp of theory than application. Although there is a lack of detailed evaluation in relation to a number of points that have been raised, the range of valid arguments that are developed and the evidence of evaluation that is apparent throughout should be sufficient to secure an A grade.**

Student B

A firm will want to take over another firm in order to benefit from economies of scale.

ⓔ This is a very brief opening paragraph, but it does launch straight into a relevant concept.

> There are many different types of economies of scale. Bulk-buying means that the firm can buy things cheaply. This means that it can cut its prices and force the competition out of the market. If the other firms become bankrupt it can put its price up and make even more money.

ⓔ This is relevant analysis of a reason for a takeover and thus earns the student some marks for analysis.

Without any competition it will be able to put more money back into the company for marketing and research and development. This will help it to make even more money.

ⓔ The brevity of the paragraphs means the student is not explaining his/her ideas fully.

Taking over another firm will mean other economies of scale. The retailer will be able to advertise more. Using television and national newspapers will help it to reach more customers and become a household name. This will improve recognition of its name and encourage more people to buy its products. It will also have the money to spend on market research, finding out exactly what its customers want. This will mean that it can make goods specifically to suit the consumers, increasing its sales even more.

ⓔ There is some further analysis of theory here, but the student is really finding many different ways to make the same point. If your essay plan (which you should develop before starting to write) only contains a list of the same or similar points, you should question whether you have interpreted the question correctly. Questions are not set to catch candidates out, but to allow them to show their understanding — so make sure that you have made the right choice of essay before starting to write.

New equipment can be bought. Investing in IT will help the retailer to improve the efficiency of its activities. Production, administration and stock control will all be improved, and so there will be less waste and inefficiency.

ⓔ The direction this answer is taking is becoming worrying. There has been no attempt to apply this answer to electrical retailers or to any other type of business. The points made so far could apply to any type of company and to firms that are just growing organically rather than through takeovers.

New methods such as kaizen and TQM can be introduced. These will lead to continuous improvement and better quality, which will, in turn, attract more customers. Higher prices can be charged if the products are of higher quality.

ⓔ This answer illustrates a common weakness in essay writing. Although it begins by discussing issues related to the question posed, it is now moving on to an associated topic and one that does not relate clearly to the question. Economies of scale are ways of improving efficiency; kaizen and TQM can also improve a firm's efficiency. However, whereas a takeover can lead to economies of scale, there is no reason why a takeover should lead to kaizen or TQM.

Just-in-time methods will also improve stock control. Goods will be ordered just in time. This will eliminate the need for warehouses. This will save costs — there will be less rent to pay, fewer employees needed and less chance of damage and theft. These savings will increase the profit of the firm. Under 'just-in-time' customers can give details of the exact product that they want. This will increase demand, allowing more profit to be made and ploughed back into research and development. Research and development will help the firm to discover consumer tastes and target new market segments.

(e) There is nothing here that is relevant to the question. It appears that the student is trying to write all he/she knows about how to improve efficiency, rather than answering the question.

In conclusion, there are many factors that a firm should consider. The main factor is economies of scale. A large firm will be able to make more money by buying in bulk, and so lower its prices. It will also help it to borrow money more cheaply, use the best marketing media, carry out detailed market research and introduce IT. New methods such as lean production can be used. With all these changes the takeover will help the firm to improve its productivity and profit.

(e) There is an attempt to bring the answer back to addressing the question in this conclusion. Much of it simply repeats previous points made, but some new points are raised.

(e) **Overall judgement: This is a disappointing answer and highlights the need to plan an essay and ensure the answer is closely focused on the question at all points. Not only does the student not focus on the business issues of takeovers and mergers, but there is also no application to the context of electrical retailers. The analysis of economies of scale would receive some reward and some credit would be given for the conclusion. However, overall this response would not earn a pass grade.**

Question 3

If organisational culture is simply 'the way we do things around here', discuss, using business examples with which you are familiar, why organisational culture is so important to business success.

(40 marks)

ⓔ The key words are 'discuss' and 'using business examples'. Make sure that you answer the question (why organisational culture is so important to business success) — don't simply write all that you know about organisational culture.

Student A

In this essay, I will begin by explaining the nature of organisational culture and the way that cultures are classified. I will then discuss why organisational culture is important for business success.

ⓔ Although not absolutely necessary, this type of introduction does set the scene and give the reader an idea of the structure of the answer.

Organisational culture is the body of informal knowledge and shared meanings and symbols that help everyone interpret and understand how to act and behave within an organisation. A key role of organisational culture is to differentiate an organisation from others and to provide a sense of identity for its members. Thus every organisation has its own unique culture, which will have been created as a result of the values of the founders, senior management and core people who built and now direct the organisation. Over time, the culture may change as new owners and senior management try to impose their own styles and preferences on the organisation or because of changing marketplace conditions. Thus, culture influences the decision-making processes, styles of management and what everyone sees as success. Interpreting and understanding organisational culture is therefore a very important activity for managers because it affects strategic development.

ⓔ The student demonstrates a sophisticated level of understanding of organisational culture and provides a clear analysis of how important it is to all organisations.

Having said that every organisation has its own culture, management theorists suggest that there are a number of different types of culture into which most organisations fit. The business guru, Charles Handy, identified four different types of organisational culture based on power and influence, what motivates people, how people think and learn, and how change should occur. These are:
• Power cultures, where a powerful individual or a small group determines the dominant culture. Power cultures are a bit like a web with a spider. Those in the web are dependent on the power of the spider. Rays of power and influence spread out from the spider who could be a single central figure or a group. An example of such an organisation is a small, entrepreneurial company, where power derives

from the founder or top person, and where a personal relationship with that individual matters more than any formal title or position. However, in some large companies, a charismatic leader like Virgin's Richard Branson might also encourage a power culture.

- Role or bureaucratic cultures, where there is an emphasis on hierarchical structures, precisely defined roles and responsibilities and detailed procedures, with coordination from the top. Such organisations value predictability and consistency, are risk averse and find it hard to adjust to change. The civil service is an example of an organisation with a bureaucratic or role culture.

- Task cultures, where the organisation's values are related to a job or project. Task cultures are usually associated with a small team approach and are apparent in network-type organisations or small organisations cooperating to deliver a project. The emphasis is on results and getting things done. Individuals are empowered with independence and control over their work. Such organisations are flexible and adaptable; the culture emphasises talent and ideas, and involves continuous team problem solving and consultation.

- Person cultures often occur in universities and in professions, such as accountancy and legal firms, where the organisation exists as a vehicle for people to develop their own careers and expertise. In these cultures, the individual is the central point. If there is a structure, it exists only to serve the individuals within it. Those involved tend to have strong values about how they will work, and they can be very difficult for the organisation to manage. For example, Cherie Blair has such a reputation as a lawyer that the reputation of her law firm focuses on her expertise as a selling point.

An additional type of culture is that of an entrepreneurial culture, which has similarities to both Handy's power and task cultures. Organisations with this type of culture tend to emphasise results and rewards for individual initiative, risk taking, quantitative and financial goals, flexible roles, and a relatively flat and flexible structure.

(e) The student provides an exceptionally clear analysis of the various classifications of organisational culture. There is some application to actual business contexts, but it would be useful if such application could be extended.

The culture of an organisation affects the mission and aims and objectives of a company and also its decision-making procedures and behaviour. It therefore has an absolutely central role in determining the purpose of a company.

(e) Although brief, this paragraph gives a good first indication of why the student judges organisational culture to be important to business success.

There is no 'right' or 'wrong' culture since the appropriate approach depends on the nature of the business and the environment in which it operates. **a** However, when mergers and takeovers occur, firms with very different cultures, even though they might be operating in similar markets and with similar technologies, are brought together, often leading to managerial confusion and failure. Differences in culture can be an important explanation of why so many mergers and takeovers fail. **b** As Google has expanded and needed a clearer structure, it has caused conflict with its 'person' style culture.

🅔 **a** The first sentence is important — that there is no right or wrong culture — but the link between this and the rest of the paragraph is not clearly made.

b The point about mergers and takeovers is spot on and illustrates another reason why organisational culture is so important to business success. Reference to actual examples of failed mergers or takeovers would have demonstrated wider reading and a greater ability to apply theory to a business context.

A successful business needs a culture that is appropriate for the environment in which it operates. A change in the external environment of a business may require profound changes in the way things are done within it. For example, if the market in which a business with a bureaucratic or role culture operates becomes more competitive, the business might find it difficult to cope. The bureaucratic culture might hinder the ability of the organisation to adapt to change because this type of culture tends to be characterised by strong resistance to change. This is natural because the fundamental values of staff will be under threat. But in addition, bureaucratic cultures tend to discourage risk taking and even penalise managers who introduce unsuccessful projects. As a result, individuals will fear failure and are likely to reject interesting or exciting new projects because they are judged too risky or uncertain.

As a result of this, a business facing significant change in its external environment may need to bring about equally significant change in its organisational culture if it is to remain successful. However, it is an excellent culture for organisations that need consistent interpretations of rules, such as the civil service.

🅔 This is an excellent example of detailed and accurate analysis leading to a clear and well-argued judgement.

In conclusion, it is not that a particular organisational culture is important to business success — just as there is no ideal style of leadership, so there is no preferred culture. What is important is that the organisational culture of a business is suited to the environment in which it operates, allowing it to react appropriately to market and other changes. A strong organisational culture means one that is internally consistent with the objectives and mission of the organisation and is suited to the external environment in which it operates, is shared by all employees, and is explicit in that it makes clear what is expected of people and how they should behave.

🅔 This is a succinct conclusion that captures the argument raised earlier in the answer and ensures that the question is addressed clearly.

ⓔ **Overall judgement: Although this answer does not make many references to real business contexts, it reaches an A grade because it demonstrates excellent knowledge and understanding of organisational culture, includes high-quality analysis of relevant issues and arrives at well-supported judgements that address the question very well.**

Student B

Organisational culture is the unwritten code that affects the attitudes and behaviour of staff, approaches to decision making and the leadership style of management.

ⓔ This is a good introduction and states clearly and succinctly what organisational culture is.

Organisational culture can be observed in a number of different ways in a company. It can be seen in the way everyday decisions and tasks are undertaken. In some organisations managers regularly walk around and talk to staff, in others managers are rarely seen. In some organisations managers communicate and consult with their staff on a routine basis, in others staff are only informed once decisions have been made. In some organisations employees have autonomy and independence and entrepreneurial activity is encouraged, in others employees are expected to follow procedures closely. Some organisational structures are decentralised and place emphasis on delegation, while others are more hierarchical and centralised. In some organisations challenging management's views is encouraged, in others this would be considered disloyal. Some organisations encourage cooperation between different groups, while others encourage a level of competitive rivalry. Professional jargon can exclude people and therefore reinforce professional cultures. Symbols — such as the range of pay scales, the size and location of managers' offices, whether they have their own secretaries, whether there are separate canteens, entrances and car parks for management and workers — indicate status within the organisation. Some patterns of behaviour become embedded in the way a company operates. For example, it may be that in a particular organisation, the only training that is considered worthwhile is on the job and employees are not seconded to college courses, perhaps because the owner is 'self-made' and values experience over education.

ⓔ This is a really interesting paragraph that provides a very good explanation, integrated with solid analysis, of what culture actually looks like in an organisation.

Organisational culture has been classified in many different ways. At one extreme is a 'them and us' culture where strict divisions exist between management and workers. At the other extreme, a more equitable culture tries to reduce barriers, with emphasis being placed on teamwork and more equal treatment of all.

ⓔ It appears that this is all the student is going to provide on the different types of cultures. As long as the rest of the answer focuses on answering the question this is not a problem — especially given the previous paragraph, which without labelling cultural styles formally, gives plenty of indication of the different types of cultures that might be apparent in organisations.

As mentioned in my introduction, organisational culture affects the leadership's style of management and it is also affected by leadership style.

Leadership styles are the manner and approach taken by the managing director in a business towards his or her staff. Their manner will affect their personal relationships with their employees. There are four main categories of leadership style — authoritarian, paternalistic, democratic and laissez-faire.

- Authoritarian leadership involves a top-down approach to communication. It tends not to involve the workforce in any decision making and tends to be controlling. It follows McGregor's Theory X style and assumes workers are not interested in work and need to be coerced to get them to put any effort in.
- Paternalistic leadership involves consulting employees although control remains firmly at the top. It is really similar to an authoritarian style but where management believes it knows what is best for its employees and tries to ensure that decisions are made with this best interest in mind.
- Democratic leadership involves two-way communication and considerable delegation. Workers are consulted about decisions. It follows McGregor's Theory Y approach and assumes workers are responsible and self-motivated individuals.
- Laissez-faire leadership is where management has little or no input and leaves things alone.

ⓔ In the first paragraph of this essay, the student states that organisational culture is affected by leadership style. This is a valid point and could well form part of his/her argument in answering the question. However, it is unclear why the student has included an analysis of leadership styles here.

As mentioned, the culture of an organisation affects, and is affected by, the style of leadership. The culture of an organisation will also affect the amount of resistance to change and therefore the ability of new leaders to impose their style or decisions on subordinates. In this sense organisational culture is vitally important to business success. If the culture prevents a new manager carrying out their role properly then the business is not going to be very successful. Equally if a weak leader is able to influence the culture of an organisation, then it is not going to be a very successful business.

ⓔ There are some valid points included in this last paragraph, but as a whole and as a conclusion it is weak and confused.

ⓔ **Overall judgement: This is a weak answer and is likely to gain no more than an E grade. The student clearly has good knowledge and understanding of what organisational culture is and how it can be identified in a business. However, the student failed to plan and structure his/her answer in order to address the question. The reference to leadership styles is relevant, but it is not linked effectively, or in detail, to organisational culture and hence does not add significantly to answering the question.**

Question 4

'You should always follow your gut instincts.' (Wayne Hemingway of the Red or Dead fashion house). Using business examples with which you are familiar, discuss whether this statement is always true in relation to business decision making.

(40 marks)

ⓔ The key words are 'Using business examples', 'discuss' and 'always true'. The question asks you to discuss whether the statement is 'always' true in relation to business decision making — remember to address that in your answer.

Student A

In this essay, I will explain decision making based on hunch or 'gut instinct' and decision making based on a scientific approach. I will then analyse the advantages and disadvantages of each system. I will finish by drawing conclusions from my analyses and evaluating whether the statement is always true.

ⓔ This introductory paragraph suggests that the answer is likely to be tightly structured and focused on the question. It also indicates that the student has a clear understanding of how he/she will demonstrate the assessment objectives of analysis and evaluation.

Decision making in any business is very important and takes place at every level of the organisation. It varies from short term to long term and from functional and tactical to strategic and corporate. Decisions are usually constrained by both internal and external factors — for example, by the finance available, the skills of the workforce, competitor activity or government policy. Most decision making includes an element of risk, but just because something is risky does not mean that it should not be pursued.

ⓔ This introduction demonstrates that the student understands the different issues involved in decision making within a business very well. However, given the time constraint in an examination, it is rather long and there has been no discussion yet of the key issues in order to address the question.

A number of different approaches to decision making are available to assist firms in this process. These range from intuitive to scientific approaches. An intuitive approach to decision making means that decisions are made on the basis of a hunch or the 'gut instincts' (mentioned in the question) of a person, which means that it is based on their personal views. This approach is more likely to be used by small businesses that are owned by a single individual or small group. The quote in the question probably refers to when Red or Dead was first set up. As a business grows, the approach can still be appropriate as long as the individual or groups involved in decision making have a great deal of experience and expertise.

A scientific approach to decision making involves using a systematic process for making decisions in an objective manner. Most scientific approaches to decision making involve five steps: setting objectives, gathering data, analysing data, selecting a strategy, and implementing and reviewing the decision.

ⓔ These two paragraphs demonstrate that the student has a very good understanding of the two different approaches to decision making. A good point is that the student has not gone into huge detail about each of the stages in scientific decision making but has indicated that he/she understands what they are.

There are a number of benefits and problems in using hunches or gut instincts when making decisions. The approach may lead to more creative and innovative decision making compared to a scientific approach. A scientific approach can be very expensive and hard to justify if there is very little risk involved. Also a scientific approach is time consuming and may mean that decisions are delayed. The data collected might be out of date or may be biased. Instead decisions may be better if they rely on the gut instincts of a manager who has a 'qualitative' understanding of the market and can anticipate a change in the trend.

However, decisions made using gut instinct or hunch are not always well informed by evidence and will often involve bias and subjectivity, which might lead to the wrong outcomes. Examples of this are siting a factory in a location that is not appropriate but is linked to the owner's childhood (such as the Mini in Oxford), and introducing a new product onto the market because competitors have done so even though competitors' sales are very low.

There are a number of benefits and problems in using a scientific approach when making decisions. Such an approach removes bias and subjectivity by ensuring that decisions are made on the basis of well-researched, factual evidence. It therefore reduces risk. By emphasising the need to set objectives (which should be SMART), it ensures that people involved in the decision-making process are aiming towards the same goals. Decisions are based on business logic, involving comparisons between alternative approaches and between pros and cons. It is likely that more than one person will be involved in the process, which will further reduce the possibility of bias. A scientific approach ensures that decisions are continually monitored and reviewed and changed if necessary, which means that mistakes can be identified quickly. It is easier to defend a decision that has been developed using good planning and cooperation with other managers than one that is just based on one person's gut instinct.

Although decisions based on rational thinking are likely to be more successful overall, it doesn't mean that the decisions made will always be the right ones. Scientific decision making can be criticised as being a rather slow process that lacks creativity and which therefore may fail to lead to innovative and different approaches. Large computer organisations such as Microsoft and Cisco Systems rarely have the chance to test out a new product fully.

ⓔ These four paragraphs demonstrate excellent analysis. The advantages and problems of each approach are clearly identified and explained. There is good linking of issues within one approach and between approaches, so that the answer is not simply a list of advantages and disadvantages but is a soundly argued analysis of the issues involved.

> The question asks whether using gut instincts (or hunches) is always the right approach to decision making. On the basis of the analyses I have provided about the intuitive and scientific approaches to decision making, my answer is NO. The most appropriate approach will depend on a number of factors and the particular context of the business. Gut instinct will be the best approach to use when quick decisions are required and there is no time to analyse the situations, when detailed data are not available or when the situation is totally unpredictable. However, if past data are reliable indicators of future changes, a scientific approach is ideal. While smaller businesses are more likely to follow the gut instincts of their owners, larger firms, because they have many departments and lots of communication and coordination issues to consider and therefore more complicated decisions to make, need a more scientific approach. Furthermore, much depends on the character of the leader or the culture of the company. An entrepreneurial risk taker (like Alan Sugar) is more likely to use hunches, while a manager (or business) that tries to avoid risk or blame is more likely to use a scientific approach in order to justify any decisions. Finally, the nature of the product or industry might influence the approach. Fashion shops such as Zara and Topshop tend to use gut feeling (partly also because of their entrepreneurial leaders). However, pharmaceutical and other health-related businesses tend to use a cautious, realistic approach.

ⓔ This is a strong conclusion that brings together the previous analysis in order to make a judgement. The judgement is decisive and the student justifies the judgement extremely well.

ⓔ **Overall judgement: This is an excellent A-grade answer that is tightly structured, demonstrates very good knowledge and understanding, and provides high-quality analysis that leads to well-argued evaluation.**

Student B

> Decisions are made either scientifically or using hunch. I will discuss both of these approaches and decide which is the best.

ⓔ This introduction suggests that the student has not read the question clearly — the question doesn't actually ask candidates to decide which the best approach is.

> Making decisions based on a hunch means using your instincts to decide. This will be OK if you have a lot of experience and knowledge of the particular thing you are deciding. The benefits of using hunches to make decisions are:
> - It requires less data.
> - It is a cheaper process.
> - It requires less time.
>
> A scientific approach uses a set procedure and makes decisions based on evidence and a logical approach. These are the stages involved:

1 Set objectives — in relation to what the business wants to achieve within a certain time.
2 Gather data — through primary and secondary research methods.
3 Analyse data — in order to provide a recommendation. One way of doing this is to use decision trees.
4 Select a strategy to pursue based on the recommendations that emerge from the data analysis.
5 Implement and review the decision. Reviewing the decision involves looking at how well the result of the decision has succeeded in achieving the initial objective.

The benefits of using a scientific approach to make decisions are:
• It provides a clear sense of direction.
• It bases decisions on objective evidence.
• It involves monitoring and reviewing the decision.

(e) These three paragraphs indicate that the student has good knowledge and understanding of the two main approaches to decision making. The problem is that the knowledge is not being applied to any business examples and there is very little analysis. The use of bullet points tends to hinder rather than encourage analysis.

The marketing model is an example of a scientific decision-making approach that ensures that marketing decisions are taken on a scientific basis. Decision tree analysis is another example of a scientific decision-making approach. This uses a diagram that resembles the branches of a tree. It maps out the different options available, the possible outcomes of these options and the points where decisions have to be made. Calculations based on the decision tree can be used to determine the best option for the business to select. 'What if?' or sensitivity analysis is another example of a scientific approach to decision making and can be used in conjunction with decision trees.

The advantages of decision trees are:
• They set out the problem clearly and encourage a logical approach to decision making.
• They encourage careful consideration of all alternatives.
• They encourage a quantitative approach and mean the process can be computerised.
• They take risk into account when making decisions.
• They are useful when similar situations have happened before, so that realistic estimates of probabilities and financial returns can be made.
• They are useful when making tactical decisions rather than strategic decisions.

The disadvantages of decision trees are:
• They ignore the constantly changing nature of the business environment.
• It is difficult to get accurate and realistic data in order to estimate probabilities.
• It is easy for managers to manipulate the data.

(e) The above three paragraphs indicate that the student has good knowledge and understanding of approaches to decision making. But it is almost as if the student has learnt the information in the hope of including it in an answer regardless of whether the question requires it.

In conclusion, the statement isn't always true because some people argue that decision making is most effective when a scientific approach is taken — for the reasons indicated above. The statement is true in some situations — when there is not much time or money and not much data available, and where the person making the decision is experienced and knowledgeable, basing decisions on a hunch might be the best thing to do.

(e) The conclusion does relate back to the question and attempts some very superficial evaluation. However, the paragraph simply restates points made earlier.

(e) **Overall judgement: The answer reads as if the student has learnt his/her notes about decision making and provided them here. There is no real attempt to address the question. Although knowledge and understanding of approaches to decision making is good, there is no attempt to apply this knowledge to business examples or to the question posed. The extensive use of bullet points means that there is very little analysis and virtually no evaluation. This is unlikely to earn a pass grade.**

Knowledge check answers

1. At the top of the hierarchy are the broad corporate aims or goals for the organisation. These are then translated into more specific but nevertheless company-wide objectives. In turn, these are translated into specific functional or departmental objectives for finance, marketing, operations and human resources. This ensures that each functional area is directing its activities to achieving the overall aims of the organisation.

2. Internal stakeholders include owners, shareholders, employers and managers.
   External stakeholders include customers, competitors, suppliers, central and local government agencies, pressure groups, bankers, trade associations and the local community.

3. Because firms producing consumer goods will expect to sell fewer items in a recession, they will cancel expansion plans that require the purchase of new machinery and plant and will delay replacing older machinery and plant, therefore affecting firms that produce capital goods.

4. The total value of a country's output over the course of a year.

5. Opportunity cost measures cost in terms of the next best alternative foregone.

6. Saving money is less attractive and people may prefer to spend rather than save.
   The cost of goods bought on credit will fall and thus demand may increase.
   Variable-rate mortgage payments and other loan repayments will fall, meaning that home owners and borrowers will have more discretionary income, which they might spend on consumer goods.

7. The price of purchasing imported raw materials will rise and, as a result, the firm's costs of production will rise. The firm might increase the price at which it sells its own products or might decide to absorb the increase in costs by reducing its profit margin. Its decision will depend on the price elasticity of demand.

8. Answers include:
   - Higher prices may mean lower sales.
   - Consumers may become more aware of price differences between brands and demand for premium brands may suffer.
   - Pressure to improve wage levels in order to maintain the level of real income may lead to industrial action by employees.
   - Suppliers may increase the price of their products, thus increasing costs of production.
   - International competitiveness may suffer if inflation in the UK is higher than elsewhere.

9. Structural, cyclical, seasonal and frictional unemployment.

10. Reorganising the firm in order to make major savings and to increase efficiency. It usually involves cutbacks in fixed overhead costs. Examples include:
    - delayering
    - in a multi-site business, closing a factory or centralising one of the departments
    - outsourcing work

11. Any two from:
    - to avoid the risk of operating in a single market
    - to take advantage of economies of scale and increasing profits
    - a desire to increase market share
    - a need to compete against international firms in order to safeguard domestic markets

12. New markets for existing products and for new products. Low production cost, including cheap labour, low land prices and less stringent government controls.

13. Supply and demand determine prices, which in turn act as signals to influence resource allocation.

14. A rise in the rate of income tax will mean people have less disposable income, which will reduce their ability to buy goods and services.
    A rise in the rate of corporation tax for small firms might deter people from setting up their own businesses.
    A rise in VAT will lead to a rise in prices, which might lead to a reduction in demand for goods and services.

15. An increase in the number of products produced will lead to a reduction in the average costs of production because the fixed costs are spread over a larger number of products; in addition, because of the ability to buy in bulk and improve efficiency, average costs will fall.

16. Tariffs; quotas; embargoes; other barriers such as technical regulations.

17. Complying with employment legislation may improve a firm's relations with its employees and improve their motivation and productivity.
    Complying with consumer protection legislation might improve the quality of products or services and might reduce waste, which in turn might reduce costs, enhance a firm's reputation and strengthen consumer loyalty.
    Complying with environmental protection legislation might enhance a business's corporate standing, which in turn can be used to help promote a company's products and services.
    Complying with health and safety legislation might have a beneficial effect on recruitment since potential employees are more likely to want to work for a firm with a good safety record.

18. Social costs include the internal or financial costs plus the external costs of an activity. Examples include:
    - The costs of operating a factory include the internal financial costs of production and the possible external costs of air and noise pollution caused by its activities.
    - The costs of operating a road haulage firm include the internal financial costs and the possible external costs of road congestion and road accidents caused by its activities.

19. Primary sector examples include: specialist machinery such as combine harvesters, mining equipment, deep-sea oil rigs,

computerised fish-locating equipment; genetically modified crops, fertilisers, pesticides.

Secondary sector examples include: production-line equipment such as robotics and computer-aided manufacture (CAM), computer-aided design (CAD); research and development; stock control; packing.

Tertiary sector examples include: communications; financial records and services such as automated teller machines; logistics design and transport; internet shopping; barcodes.

20 Fair competition is a situation where firms compete on equal terms in a way that offers consumers the best choice of products and prices.

Unfair competition is a situation where firms do not compete fairly, but act in a way that restricts consumer choice in the short or long run.

21 Delayering means removing a layer of management from the organisation hierarchy.

22 A management buyout (MBO) is where the managers of a business buy out the existing shareholders in order to gain ownership and control of the business or part of the business.

23 Strategic decisions concern the general direction and overall policy of a firm. They have significant long-term effects and can be high risk because the outcomes are unknown and will remain so for some time. For example, if a firm's goal is market dominance, it will have to decide whether to expand by acquisition or by organic growth.

Tactical decisions tend to be short to medium term and are concerned with specific areas rather than overall policy. They are calculated and their outcome is more predictable. For example, if a product's sales are below target, a firm might decide to cut the price and/or run a sales promotion.

24 Strengths might include: reputation for quality products, innovative, highly skilled staff, modern equipment, efficient structure.

Weaknesses might include: poor reputation, weak product portfolio, high staff turnover and absenteeism, communication problems, cash-flow problems.

Opportunities might include: change in attitudes towards the environment, low wages and high unemployment, falling exchange rate, new emerging markets.

Threats might include: downturn in business cycle, high levels of competition, technological change makes plant obsolete, adverse pressure group activity.

25 Stages in contingency planning include:
- recognising the need for contingency planning
- distinguishing between critical and non-critical issues
- listing all possible crisis scenarios and analysing their impact
- searching for ways to prevent each crisis
- formulating plans for dealing with each crisis
- simulating each crisis and the operation of each plan

26 Answers include:
- Affects relationships with employees — loyalty, respect, fear.
- Affects extent to which delegation takes place.
- Affects extent to which consultation takes place.

All of which affect motivation and productivity.

27 Change management is the anticipation, organisation, introduction and evaluation of modifications to business strategy and operations.

28 Marketing-orientated organisations place heavy emphasis on meeting the needs of their customers and are continually alert to changes in the market (e.g. Virgin).

Production-orientated organisations place an emphasis on good engineering and high quality in production (e.g. Dyson). Technology-orientated organisations define themselves in terms of the technology they exploit (e.g. Polaroid).

29 Answers include:
- investment appraisal
- cost–benefit analysis
- critical path analysis
- ratio analysis
- decision tree analysis

30 A stakeholder is an individual or group with a direct interest in the activities and performance of an organisation; stakeholders include shareholders as well as employees, consumers, the local community and suppliers.

A shareholder is a person or organisation that owns a part (share) of a business.

31 A project manager's focus is to plan, organise and manage the execution of the project.

A project champion, although not a member of the project team, strives to help the project succeed by advocating and promoting the benefits of pursuing the project, actively seeking support from management and other organisational leaders, and assisting the project when it encounters barriers, such as funding constraints or problems with resource allocation.

32 A flat team structure is often the most appropriate structure for implementing and managing change successfully.

33 Competitors' actions; changes in the economic environment.